FRIENDS
WITH
FOUR LEGS

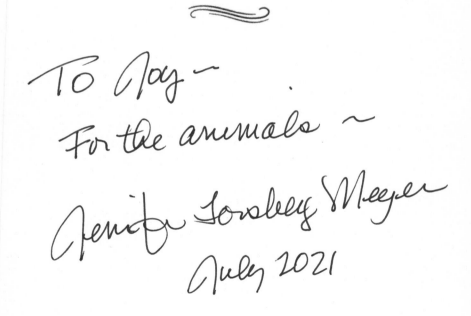

To Joy ~
For the animals ~

Jenifer Forsberg Meyer
July 2021

FRIENDS
WITH
FOUR LEGS

The Joys &
Diversions
of a Life
With Animals

JENNIFER
FORSBERG
MEYER

Friends with Four Legs:
The Joys & Diversions of a Life with Animals
Copyright © 2021 by Jennifer Forsberg Meyer
All rights reserved.

Meyer, Jennifer Forsberg

Friends with Four Legs: The Joys & Diversions of a Life with Animals/Jennifer Forsberg Meyer

1. Animals. 2. Memoir. 3. Essays.

First printing, 2021

ISBN: 978-1-737084-20-4

Cover design by Kelli Ann Morgan
Author photo by Sheri Scott Photography
Glyphs by Freepik.com. This book has been designed using resources from Freepik.com
Interior book design by Bob Houston eBook Formatting

Published in the United States of America

DEDICATION

For my mother, who taught me how to love animals, and my father, who helped make it all possible.

For my husband, Hank, who loves animals at least as much as I do and supports me in everything.

For my daughter, Sophie Elene, who taught me how to tame kittens.

And for all my four-legged friends, who bring such joy and whimsy to my life.

FOREWORD

I have been a great fan of Jenny Meyer for two decades. We met via a conference call about an end-of-century *Practical Horseman* section that we and another equestrian journalist were asked to write. When this magazine assignment was completed, Jenny and I found that our emails swaps continued as email pen-pal correspondence, one that continues to this day.

Over the years, Jenny has sent me many of her stories and musings capturing slices of life with her family and particularly their interactions with their dogs, cats, goats, horses...indeed, a delightful Noah's Ark full of domesticated quadrupeds. Her book became old-home week when I became reacquainted with Buddy the goat and his pasture-mate pony Brego, Sadie from irrepressible puppyhood to maturity, daughter Sophie's first pony, Diamond, and the rest of the Meyer menagerie.

Friends With Four Legs brings to mind a parable from J.D. Salinger's *Raise High The Roofbeams, Carpenter.* A Chinese nobleman asked a horseman friend to recommend someone who could find superior horses for him. The friend suggested a man named Kao. Accepting the task, Kao returned to report that he had found a dun-colored mare. However, the animal turned out to be a coal-black stallion. Much displeased, the nobleman complained to his friend that Kao made a mess of the job. "Why, he cannot even distinguish a beast's color or sex," the nobleman fumed. "What on earth can he know about horses?" The friend replied that Kao focuses on essence, observing things he should look at and neglecting those things that are irrelevant. And when the horse arrived, it turned out indeed to be a superlative animal.

The Salinger story comes to mind because Jenny's book shows a deep understanding of essentials, especially the lessons they can teach us if only we listen.

In her insightful words: "Animals remind us that the basics of life matter far more than this technological treadmill. They guide us back to the natural world, the one we long for—often without even realizing it—when we get too far drawn into the vortex of life as it is in the twenty-first century.

"Animals represent simple, eternal virtues: living in the moment, honoring each day, tending to the bonds that make life meaningful. They stick by their friends, and they find ways to live peaceably in groups. By the simple fact of their own true natures, our four-legged friends challenge us to take a page from their humble books...and become better humans in the process."

Jenny also asks us to look inside ourselves. "I love my animals unconditionally; I accept them just as they are. That feels good for them, and for me—a win-win situation. So my question is, Why is this so much harder to do with the humans in our lives? Why do we persist in expecting change from them—even changes we know in our hearts they're not going to make? [We could] give people the same break we give our pets. Live and let live, and enjoy them anyway. We do it naturally for animals, but resist it with humans. Yet it's so freeing to release ourselves from wishing things could be different."

The Elizabethan poet Sir Philip Sydney told us that a poem should "delight and instruct." You'll find both qualities within these pages: the joys and emotional fulfillment that pet ownership brings (as well as the heartbreak of losing a beloved animal to illness or old age) and lessons of responsibility and maturity that they can teach us.

If I were sending anyone to find me a horse or any other (if I may coin a word) quadru-pet, I'd send Jenny Meyer.

Steven D. Price
New York, NY
January, 2019

CONTENTS

INTRODUCTION

Animals enrich our lives. They improve our health, sweeten our mental outlook, even spur our spiritual growth. The texture of my days would be so much plainer without the amusement, mystery, poignancy, and joy that my four-legged friends have given me.

Because you're reading this, I know you agree. Not everyone does, however. And, in fairness, I do understand their objections. Animals are a bother. They tie you down. They're messy, and often expensive. (Sometimes exceedingly so.)

All true. To which I say, many of the same downsides apply to children, spouses, even friends. It seems the best things in life have a "price tag" attached. So the real question is, Are our friends with four legs worth it?

I believe they are.

This book celebrates that belief. It's my love letter to the animals that have graced my life so far. There have been many: dogs, cats, horses, ponies, goats, even the occasional wild creature, observed from a distance. Each has left me richer in some real if intangible way.

I owe my love of animals to my parents, who encouraged this affinity in all five of their daughters. I can't remember not having a dog in our lives. There was patient Seto, a beloved German

Shepherd, our first dog. The mutt Lunky, so named (by me, at age six) because "he lunks on your foot." And Rocky, a gentle, patient Greyhound that became a horse substitute for my sisters and me in our pre-equine period.

We also had cats, even though my mother disapproved of them. No fan of feline nature, she especially disliked the way cats leap onto countertops when they think you're not looking. And litter boxes? She loathed them.

And yet...when her three youngest daughters were at the age when a little ball of fur is the most desirable thing in the world, she let each one of us have a kitten, and she let us keep those kittens in the house (with litter boxes). I can still see those cats now in my mind's eye: Midnight, Angel, and Cutie-Pie. Thus began my lifelong love affair with cats.

My mother did approve of horses. She planted the seed in our young minds that we would someday own one. Her own horse experience was limited, but she knew we needed something to anchor us and fire our imaginations. As an Air Force family, we moved...a *lot*. Entering a new school (which I did every grade until high school) was easier when you had your good horse books to keep you company until you made new friends. Plus the dream of actually owning horses gave us something thrilling to look forward to.

Though unfamiliar with horses, my father supported these dreams. In fact, when my older twin sisters were thirteen, he found a dealer and purchased our family's first horse. Then, with no prior experience in the saddle, he rode that buckskin gelding several miles over back roads to our rural home in Waco, Texas.

When Dunbar turned out to be a runaway (darn those horse traders, anyway), my mom found the twins an older, gentler mare, and my dad managed to fetch Missy home, too. When Dad was transferred back to California, we had to sell Missy, but the plan remained to buy property and settle down permanently—and get horses again—when he retired from the service.

Except...my younger sisters and I, chomping at the bit for "our very own" horse, couldn't wait. When I was twelve and they were ten and eight, we hatched a plan. A local pony breeder was sponsoring a raffle to promote her farm's upcoming dispersal sale. The drawing for the prize—a weanling pony colt—was to be held at the auction, the old "must be present to win" ploy. Free raffle tickets were dispensed with every purchase at the neighborhood grocery store, just a short walk down the block from us.

By the time auction day rolled around, the horse-crazy Forsberg girls had accumulated more than a hundred raffle tickets in the hopes of winning that scrawny little colt. We begged our mother to take us to the auction—just for the drawing, mind you, and not to purchase a pony at the auction itself. Of course not!

As it turned out, we didn't win the raffle colt that day. But we did, miracle of miracles, come home with a pony—a gentle, mature, rideable pony. A pony our mother bid on and bought for us as we huddled next to her on a bale of straw, barely able to breathe. A pony we put in our suburban backyard for a couple of months, where she devoured all the grass—and my mom's rose bushes—until we could find a place to board her. A pony my mother bought, quite simply, because she couldn't bear to see her daughters disappointed.

A year later, my family finally acquired that much-longed-for property, ten acres in California's Sierra foothills. My younger sisters and I, brimming with horse-book knowledge, planned to put a small pasture here, a larger pasture there, and maybe (please, Dad?) a little barn in between.

All of it came to pass. It stretched our family's budget, but my parents knew instinctively that having and loving a horse is a safety valve for girls navigating that tricky passage from childhood to womanhood. "Just get 'em horses," my dad used to say. "Get 'em horses and the horses will do the rest."

This proved especially true for me. I was a nerdy teen with glasses and braces. What made it bearable was Tigress, my young Thoroughbred mare. She made it not matter that I wasn't popular at school and didn't date. I had her to love and care for—a wholly acceptable tradeoff.

On Tigress I discovered the joys of galloping across the countryside, jumping over anything that blocked our way. Never, before or since, have I experienced such freedom, power, and confidence. These were glorious feelings for a teenage girl, and I'm so thankful to my parents—and that wonderful mare—for making them possible.

Time passed. I grew up, went to college, met and married my husband, became a journalist. Much of my writing has been about animals, and now that my husband and I have raised a daughter of our own, we can appreciate the value of four-legged friends from a parent's standpoint, too. My husband (who was also raised with pets) and I have tried to give Sophie all the advantages that a life with animals can offer.

I only hope we did it a fraction as well as my own parents. They got it right, and the lessons about love I learned as a result have shaped my life.

Yes, animals are a bother and a hassle and an expense. Their love always comes at a price, it's true…but that price is always worth it.

Part I. Animals: A Lifetime Bond

The best things in life aren't things.
~Art Buchwald

Four-legged friends change our lives forever. We remember our first pet—the one we likely begged for—plus those that came after, including the scraggly ones we rescued. The unique characteristics of each bonded the animal to us in ways some people find hard to understand, given that it was "just a dog" or "just a cat."

Just a one-of-a-kind friend, in reality.

The horse-crazy among us remember that first beloved pony—the one more valuable, in our eyes, than Secretariat. For girls, especially, the role of a horse looms large at the time of life when a constant, nonjudgmental friend is essential.

We remember them all—the brief visitors in our lives and the animals that stayed until their time on Earth was up, teaching us lessons about life and death, joy and heartache.

Here are a few of my dearest memories of my own four-legged friends.

Chapter 1: Savage Love

H is name was Spunky, but it could as easily have been Slasher the way he wielded those claws. My hands and arms and ankles were threaded with tiny scabs back in the day, when my family owned this magnificent cat.

A Siamese-Himalayan cross, beautiful Spunky had medium-length fur, soft brown points, and blue eyes. We acquired him too young, though I didn't understand that at the time. His owner told me he was weaned, eating kitten chow, and using a litter box at five weeks. "He's ready for a new home," she said.

What I discovered later is that kittens use those critical last few weeks together with their litter-mates—until they're at least eight weeks of age, ideally—learning to pull their punches.

"Scratch me, and I'll scratch you" is the code of the kitten. Miss this early training and a wee one never properly learns to keep his claws sheathed during play.

Not that we didn't try to teach him ourselves. My daughter, seven when we adopted Spunky, would immobilize him with one hand while gently rubbing his forehead with the other. She called this method of taming, in her second-grader wisdom, "Giving him a seizure."

My sister Sherry loves to tell the story of the time she kitty-sat for us when my husband, daughter, and I went away for the weekend. Spunky, then about eight weeks old, slept in Sherry's guest bathroom with a blanket and litter box. In the morning, my sister brought him to her bedroom and shut the door to keep track of him while she dressed for work.

Feeling fresh and fierce, the kitten attacked.

"He would hide under the bed, then dart out and grab my ankle, then race back under the dust ruffle," my sister reported upon our return. "Makes it hard to get your lipstick on. I was almost late for work."

"We use a spray bottle for that. I meant to give it to you," I replied, lamely. "A quick squirt discourages that behavior."

"Now you tell me!"

I don't think she's ever fully forgiven me.

Spunky calmed down as he grew older (and was neutered). He matured into a luxurious pet. He looked not like a house cat but more like a miniature snow leopard. His lovely coat, rabbit-fur soft and subtly shaded, made him practically an interior-design accessory. I called him my carpet ornament.

He exuded regal charm. He would stroll into the room languidly, head and tail held high. We greeted him accordingly.

"Hello, Your Majesty."

He could be flirtatious. When he wanted attention, he would draw close, fling one front leg around my lower calf and hold on, this time without the claws. He wanted petting. It was his way of saying, "Hey, baby."

I remember thinking I needed to quit my job and clear my schedule so I could devote full time to adoring him.

We had him just two years. In Spunky's second summer with us, a feral cat and her kitten took up residence in our garage. It took us a while to figure out how to capture them. In the meantime, Spunky—lacking proper feline socialization—felt traumatized with these cat strangers under his roof.

Though he had always come in at night, one night—while the feral cats were still in our garage—he didn't. I'll never forget calling him forlornly from our back deck, under the light of an ill-omened gibbous moon. Awake off and on all night, I listened in vain for the slight sound of the cat door downstairs, opening.

When he still wasn't home the next morning, I knew he would never be back. Too many predators out at night that would notice my light-colored snow leopard.

Grief consumed me. It seemed so cruel that a creature you loved so much could be right there with you one day, but—poof!—gone forever the next.

Then one night a week later I felt him land lightly on the foot of our bed and work his way quickly up between my husband and me. I bolted upright and threw the covers back to discover...that it had been a dream. A fervent wish-dream.

A nightmare in reverse, actually.

More time passed, softening the edges of my grief. In the fall of that year, we acquired two new cats, litter-mates Leo and Locket. Fully socialized "teenagers" when we adopted them, neither has ever so much as shown us a claw. I love them both dearly, my gentle black cats, yet still I sometimes dream of my fierce snow leopard.

My Spunky.

Chapter 2: Dog on a Mission

Animals generally come into our lives by design, but not always. Sometimes they turn up on their own, and in those instances it can almost seem as if they're on a mission.

Such was the case with a Labrador Retriever/German Shepherd mix that arrived at our doorstep one day in the early 1990s. An unneutered male, he was young and healthy, mostly black with warm brown points.

When he saw my husband, Hank, and me for the first time, he almost literally bent over backwards to ingratiate himself, "smiling" and wagging and collapsing his slender, athletic body into a tight coil first one way, then the other.

It's hard to resist a display like that.

We weren't in the market for another dog, however. We already had two largish mutts, the neutered male litter-mates Zack and Gabe, our white Golden Retriever/German Shepherd mixes.

Two was plenty, and we stood firm in that conviction. But you know how convictions go. They're easy to make and keep in the abstract. In the face of a real, live, exceptionally personable dog…they wilt.

Watching this dog in his curlicue routine, I remarked without thinking, "His name should be Noodle." A mistake, of course—

giving him a name. After that, he seemed even more like a part of the family, and I had to keep reminding myself we were keeping him just until his owners turned up.

I called around to neighbors and checked in the newspaper; no one was missing this particular dog. In the meantime, Noodle fit himself seamlessly in with Zack and Gabe. In fact, our two dogs seemed to like his personality as much as Hank and I did.

"I'll find someone at work who'll take him," I promised my husband. At the time, I was editor/publisher of a California-based performance-horse magazine. Surely someone in the office there—good animal people, all—would want such a nice dog.

My plan was to offer to pay to have him neutered before he went to his new family.

"You'll appreciate that, Noodle," I assured him. "Make a new man of you."

Settle you down, I added to myself. *You'll be able to enjoy—and stay put in—your new home.*

He gave me an especially intelligent look, and I decided on the spot that "Noodle" wasn't the right name with which to market him to an adoptive family.

"We need something better for such a brainy, handsome dog," I told him. "For promotional purposes, you will now be known as *Newton.*"

Over the next few days, I worked tirelessly on the magazine's art director, who I knew was a particularly soft touch with animals. Her resistance was beginning weaken when Noodle suddenly up and disappeared, just as mysteriously as he had come.

And here's where the story gets odd. He turned up again a day later, with a "gift" for us. He delivered to our doorstep a half-grown puppy, as cute and winsome as any I had ever seen.

Now, before I go on, I should clarify that I fully understand the concept of anthropomorphism—the ascribing of human characteristics to animals. I try to avoid engaging in it myself. If, however, I slip over that line now, describing this next scene, all I can say is, you had to be there.

The puppy looked to be something like a Dachshund/German Shepherd mix, about six months old. She was medium-sized, short-legged, and cinnamon-brown in color, with just a whisper of black around her eyes, ears, and muzzle.

As I watched in astonishment, she sat like an obedient first-grader, ears back humbly, while Noodle went into curlicue overdrive.

"Isn't she *darling?*" said his body language. "Just *adorable?* I know you'll love her, because I already love her, and one day she's going to be my WIFE."

I was glad Hank wasn't home. I needed time to think. Donna, the art director, was still waffling on adopting the dog she knew as "Newton," and if she pooped out on me, we would now have *four* dogs.

Only...that's not how this story turned out. After settling the puppy with us, Noodle disappeared once more, and we never saw him again. Maybe he went on a recruiting trip, seeking more members for his harem, and got waylaid at someone else's house.

Or perhaps his original owners found him and took him home. (And, one can hope, neutered him.)

Or maybe bringing the puppy to us was his mission in the first place. I don't know.

In any event, Heidi, as we named her, joined our family permanently and lived with us the rest of her life. She was a wonderful dog. When our daughter Sophie came along and grew old enough to appreciate our various pets, Heidi was one of her favorites. I remember her hugging the dog affectionately, cooing in her baby voice, "Heid'n, Heid'n."

Yes, a lot of sweet memories surrounding little Heidi.

So, thank you, Noodle, wherever you are.

Chapter 3: More Than a Dog

S ometimes a dog is more than a dog, at least in the eyes of the little girls who love him. I'm thinking of Rocky, a Greyhound that graced my life more than fifty years ago in Ruidoso, New Mexico. My mother had surprised her five daughters by bringing home a small white puppy with a patch of brown over one eye and another over his tail. When we girls learned this gangly baby was a Greyhound (pups of this breed actually look more like little Great Danes), we immediately wanted to name him Rocket—for the speed we were sure he would oneday have.

My mother, wanting something more elegant for such an elegant breed, suggested Marquis. In the end, we named our new puppy Rocket Marquis Forsberg, and called him Rocky.

Our first adventure with Rocky involved nearly killing him. Noticing fleas on his tender, pink-skinned hide, we sprinkled on flea powder without noticing the fine print that said, "Do NOT apply to Greyhound puppies." (Particularly thin-skinned, Greyhounds are highly sensitive to chemicals and pesticides.)

Little Rocky survived that ordeal to become the darling of our household. He was playful and highly intelligent, yet completely submissive to humans. Like all the pets I recall from childhood, he "belonged" most ardently to my mother, who provided all his meals and was generous with the table scraps.

He lived in the house with us, and was clean, quiet, and reliably housebroken. Though he soon grew to a height of about thirty inches at the withers, he retained his puppyish wrigglyness, displaying it each morning and whenever we came home from an outing. His two most notable physical characteristics were his long, beautiful face and his deep, deep heartgirth—the signature trait of a dog that can hit a speed of forty-five miles per hour in six strides. (Only the cheetah can accelerate faster.)

He loved to run, and we loved to watch him. By the time Rocky was full grown, we had moved back to Roswell, where my father was stationed with the Air Force. There, my dad would load Rocky and my sisters and me into his rattletrap van and drive out to the desert, wending his way along near-deserted roads until we found ourselves in the middle of nowhere. Then we would set Rocky loose and he would take off, looking for jackrabbits. A short time later, we would see him flying along the horizon in pursuit of a speeding hare.

He never caught his prey, but he always came back happy, his tongue lolling from his mouth, his sweet face almost smiling. "Good dog!" we told him. And that's exactly what he was.

He also served as a substitute horse in that time when my younger sisters and I were lacking the real thing. We would put him on a leash and guide him "in hand" over a series of jumps cobbled together out of lawn furniture and a broom handle or two. He was patient and willing with all this foolishness—and a rather nifty jumper.

I also recall a scheme I hatched to render him even more horse-like, at least in terms of his gear. I had seen the harnesses that some dogs wear instead of collars. Some horses wear harnesses, I reasoned, so our Rocky must have one of these leather contraptions to be buckled into, just like a horse.

I finagled my way to the pet store, where I bought the largest dog harness they had. When we got home, however, I discovered the girth strap was about three times too short to span Rocky's mighty chest.

"Rocket Marquis, your heartgirth is like Man O War's," I told him proudly, tossing the harness aside.

In the early 1960s, our family moved back to California, part of the ongoing to-ing and fro-ing the Air Force requires of its families. We settled in Elk Grove, just south of Sacramento. A few years later, my dad retired from the service and we began building the home—on ten acres in the Sierra foothills—where my sisters and I would finally have our horses.

Problem was, we had sold our house in Elk Grove and were going to live in an apartment while the new house was being built. And Rocky couldn't come with us.

It was agonizing.

We found him an adoptive home on a farm, hoping he would appreciate the room to roam. Now that I know more about Greyhounds, I realize he probably would've chosen to stay with his family in a tiny apartment over being separated to live with others on a farm—no matter how large.

We visited him several times at his new home. His adoptive family clearly loved him, and Rocky seemed content.

That said, I can't help but think that we probably broke his great big heart—at least until he made the adjustment. There may not have been a workable alternative at the time, but it still hurts to think of it, all these years later.

Because Rocky was more than a dog.

Chapter 4: A Horse by Any Other Name

H is nickname, they said, was Toy. They showed him in pony jumper classes under the name Little Present. And though it was love at first sight when we bought this Arabian/Mustang cross for our then ten-year-old daughter, we just couldn't bring ourselves to call this handsome black gelding...Toy.

Yes, he was a pony, technically. But at just under 14.2 hands, he was more like a small horse. Plus he had an elegant head with large, liquid eyes, and a noble bearing. And although he was kind, there was a reserve about him, sort of a dignified air. He wasn't an in-your-pocket type of horse. Clearly, he was not a Toy.

Still, my daughter and I agonized. Is it kosher to change a horse's name? I mean, will the horse care if you do? Do horses even know their own names? Or do they think their names are Son, Old Girl, Good Boy—whatever they hear most often?

It's hard to say. But no matter what names may mean to a horse, fussing over them has been something the people in my family have always done.

As with our very first family horse, when I was a child in the mid-1960s. Sherry, a pretty chestnut pony mare with a flaxen mane and tail, seemed well-suited to her name, but there was a problem. One of the five Forsberg girls was also named Sherry. It made for some confusion.

As when my youngest sister, Caroline, intent on having a certain special picture taken, called out, "With Sherry! With Sherry!" Flattered, Sherry-the-person obligingly posed with the seven-year-old, after which Caroline whispered, so as not to hurt her big sister's feelings, "The pony! I want one with *the pony.*"

Our family's photo collection still includes both shots, one of Caroline smiling next to her big sister, and one of Caroline smiling a bigger smile next to the pony.

Sherry-the-pony (as we came to call her) became Caroline's exclusive mount as we began adding other horses to our family collection. A part-Arabian mare was next. She bore a "DL" brand on her shoulder; her seller told us her name was Dragon Lady.

Dragon Lady! That would never do. Sensitive and smooth-gaited, the mare needed something in keeping with her status as a dream-come-true for sister Mary. Then ten, Mary never gazed at that horse without stars in her eyes. We spent days deciding what to call her. Finally, Mary settled on Showgirl, a name befitting the mare's high spirit and flashy cream color.

A year later, my own first horse, a green-broke Thoroughbred mare, came with the name Tigress. Though the name didn't really suit her (Kitten would've been more like it), somehow it stuck, and I never even thought about changing it. Go figure.

Fast forward some forty-odd years, to when my daughter and I found ourselves fussing over a name for Toy. Both ardent *Lord of the Rings* fans, Sophie and I had read the books and watched the hugely successful films multiple times. Now we remembered the horse that saved the hero, Aragorn, after a fall down a mountainside. Brego was a dark, handsome, serious horse. Noble.

"Thy name is kingly," Aragorn tells him at one point.

Hmmm. Kingly. That seemed about right to both Sophie and me. So Toy became Brego, and it's been his name ever since.

And if the change has bothered him at all, he's keeping it to himself.

Chapter 5: Sure-Footed Saviors

How important is the right kind of horse? When it comes to your family, it's all-important. This proved true in the early 1990s, when my husband's new Quarter Horse was put to the test.

Back then, Hank and I each had a horse of our own. Though my husband had rarely ridden before meeting me, his natural athleticism and empathy with animals enabled him to bond well with Dusty, a quiet, mousy-dun Quarter Horse gelding I had hand-picked to be his first mount. At 16.1 hands high and well-muscled, Dusty was imposing to look at but friendly, unflappable, and easy to ride. Perfect for a beginner.

My equine partner was Gunner, another good-natured Quarter Horse. A sleek, 16-hand-high chestnut with a flaxen mane and tail, Gunner was a looker who made my heart go pitty-pat. Solid under saddle, he was as good out on the trail as he was practicing endless circles in the arena.

The four of us—Hank on Dusty and I on Gunner—had enjoyed a few rides together around our rural neighborhood. Then my longtime friend and farrier, Ray Fine, offered to take us on one of his signature horse-camping trips.

I jumped at the chance. Had I known then what I know now, I also would've grilled Ray about the difficulty of our intended route. These days, I could've gone online and discovered it was recommended exclusively "for the fit and brave." Instead, blissfully ignorant, I began preparations for our excursion to beautiful Raymond Lake, just off the Pacific Crest Trail in the Mokelumne Wilderness of the Sierra Nevada.

When we unloaded our horses at the trailhead that lovely summer morning, everything was just as I had envisioned it. Green meadows rolled out in every direction, with towering cottonwood trees and broad dirt paths. Only, as I soon discovered, this was just the staging area. Our real journey—the part for which T-shirts ("I Survived A Ray Fine Trail Ride") actually exist—was a series of high-mountain switchbacks. These cut into the steep sides of the volcanic rock that leads up to the 9,000-foot-elevation lake, and they are heart-stopping. They reminded me of the walls of the Grand Canyon. They also made me wish I and my novice-level-equestrian husband were riding sure-footed mules. Yes, our geldings were good guys, but still…mules stick like glue.

And I noted that Ray himself was riding a mule.

The trail on those switchbacks had to be wider than eighteen inches, but that's how I remember it. I'm also sure the drop-off at the trail's edge wasn't a sheer plunge of five hundred feet, but that's what I still see in my mind's eye, decades later.

Talk about high anxiety. Forget the scenery; my eyes were glued to the trail, my mind yammering nonstop. Will the horses see that rock coming up? (No room for stumbling, here.) Will they cross this trickle of water without side-stepping? (Nowhere to step.) Will they keep their composure if—heaven forbid!—we meet backpack-laden hikers coming the opposite way?

Over the pounding of my heart, I could hear Hank chatting amiably with Ray. Oblivious to all that could go wrong, he was simply enjoying the fresh air, the scenic vistas, the companionship of his horse. As the moments stretched into what seemed an eternity, I began to appreciate his horse even more than he did. Dusty was a trouper, all right. The ideal beginner's mount. And Gunner was equally solid. I tried to concentrate on this thought, carefully avoiding words like startle, plummet, and airlift.

At one point, the pack mule Ray was leading just in front of Hank and Dusty slipped while switching back to the next bit of trail. I watched the animal's hind legs scramble over the edge for an instant before regaining purchase on the narrow path. I learned that time really does slow down at such moments. Today, I can still picture those dislodged stones making their slow-motion tumble over the edge and cascading down, down, d-o-w-n....

When we finally reached the top, my relief was a surge of adrenaline. We made it! But the jubilation wilted at the realization there was no way of return other than back over those cliffsides. Still, I managed to enjoy the last, easy mile to Raymond Lake, our fireside meal, and the overnight stay in pup tents.

The next morning, after standing tied all night, the horses were fresh. Mine, alarmingly, was bucking in place. But both Dusty and Gunner settled to their work like pros, and we made the return trip without mishap—other than my palpitations.

For years after, Ray and his wife, Linda, split their sides telling about the time Ray took the fancy-pants journalist on a trail ride—and about scared the pants off her. Hank is never a part of this narrative, and for that I'm grateful. It means he felt so safe and secure on his horse, it never occurred to him to worry.

Yes, we survived a Ray Fine trail ride, thanks to Ray himself and our own good geldings. For being just as reliable as mules that day, thank you, Gunner. Thank you, Dusty.

Chapter 6: Silver Linings

I think often how lucky I am to live where I do, in the house my husband built on acreage, where we've enjoyed a rural life for over forty years now. I also marvel at the serendipity of life, because if it hadn't been for one of the most painful experiences I've ever had, we wouldn't be living where we are now.

The year was 1976. Hank and I, married just three years, lived on the Flying C Ranch in California's El Dorado County, just east of Sacramento. The Flying C belonged to Larry Cameron, a wealthy landowner who had developed nearby Cameron Park and hobnobbed with Raquel Welch and other celebrities in his heyday.

The Flying C's outbuildings had been converted into tiny, humble apartments, one of which was just our size, rent-wise. Still in use, the ranch's large, old-fashioned barn housed my first horse, the mare Tigress. I had talked Mr. Cameron into boarding her for me in return for barn chores—I fed his two old palominos for him twice a day.

At one point during our time there, I decided to breed Tigress. I had owned her since she was three and I, thirteen. Now she was thirteen, and I wanted a foal from her to guard against that time when she would be too old to ride. She was my four-legged soul mate; I figured only something carrying her blood could ever come close to replacing her.

I pored over stallion ads. Deliberately, I chose a handsome black Quarter Horse, stout and well-muscled in all the places where my mare was a bit light. Best of all, he lived nearby—key to someone on my modest budget.

Well. Exasperating details aside, just know that it took two years and many attempts to get that mare in foal. Between years one and two, the stallion and his owners relocated to Oregon, which meant we had to rent a trailer, haul Tigress up there, and then—after she had finally conceived—fetch her back.

Still, I was thrilled. By the time she was about nine months along (in an eleven-month equine gestation), Hank and I had built a little place of our own on one acre. Tigress had a decent paddock and a tiny run-in shed. With everything set, I could hardly wait.

Then Tigress aborted the foal.

It still hurts to remember that night. After the veterinarian had finished cleaning up my mare and left, I turned Tigress back into her paddock. She nickered softly. She knew she had had a baby. She was calling for it. Stricken, I wrapped my arms around her neck and sobbed into her tangled mane.

By this time, Hank had had his fill of horse breeding. Kind soul that he is, though, he couldn't bear my disappointment.

"Just go buy another horse," he said, in his wonderfully practical way.

And so I did. But then two horses on one acre began to feel crowded. With a knack for sussing out wonderful properties, my mother found us a bargain of a deal on twenty acres at the western edge of the county, where my former carpenter husband could build us a home.

Thus here we are today, in this place perfect for raising an animal-loving daughter. If we hadn't moved when we did, as a consequence of Tigress' lost foal, we would never have been able to afford it later, given the trajectory of Northern California property values.

So that's how one of the saddest days of my life led to many of the happiest. That odd fact—of bad things turning to good—is something I've tried to keep in mind whenever something goes wrong.

More important, I've tried to teach it to my daughter.

As when we shopped for her first pony, when Sophie was eight. We had brought home a little Welsh mare on trial, but it didn't work out. Sophie, who had already begun bonding with the cute chestnut, was heartbroken.

"Honey," I said, "this just means your real pony is still out there somewhere, waiting for you. She's probably stomping her foot, saying, 'Don't keep that pony! *I'm* supposed to be your pony!'"

I could see the wheels in Sophie's head beginning to turn, so I pressed on.

"We've just got to find her. I wonder what color she is…maybe black? Palomino? Buckskin?"

Sophie's disappointment evaporated as she began imagining ponies in various colors. And in fact it was a wonderful little buckskin that turned out to be waiting for us to find her.

As soon as fortune cleared the way.

Chapter 7: Little Orphan Annie

S mall dogs are special. I've owned and loved dogs of all sizes, but somehow the littlest ones really bring out my maternal instincts. Maybe it's akin to how we naturally feel more protective over a (small) toddler as compared to a (larger) teen.

Whatever the case, the best example of it for me was with Annie, a small dog that came into my life one day in the middle of winter. She was meant to be a companion for my mother; my sisters and I hoped a little dog might encourage Mom to get up and out more.

To find just the right pooch, I had put the word out among staffers at the California-based performance-horse magazine I published at the time. I specified I was seeking a small, short-haired, fully housebroken adult dog. Before long, a former employee brought in a candidate I described in my journal as "the cutest little Toy Fox Terrier you've ever seen."

She was about four or five years old, a sleek nine pounds, white with black spots. One ear stood up smartly; the other flopped. She was shy but friendly and sweet, and desperate to latch onto someone.

Her previous owner had left her unclaimed at a veterinary clinic. She had had an ear infection and some scruffy skin condition; why anyone would abandon such an appealing dog for that or any reason is still a mystery to me.

She had only just been spayed in preparation for going to a new home, so I wondered if perhaps she was a breeding animal who was no longer needed.

I named her Annie, and she was to be my mother's 72nd-birthday present. In the letter of introduction that Annie "wrote" to my mother (with my help), she said she had simple gifts to offer, gifts that were "at the root of all happiness in this world: friendship, loyalty, companionship, love. Unconditional love of the purest kind."

Annie signed the letter with her paw print.

To our disappointment, however, the match didn't take. Our frail mother felt the responsibility of a dog might be too much for her at that time, so Annie came back to me and my husband.

"What are we going to do with her?" I asked Hank, as Annie regarded us with her gentle, deer-like eyes.

"We're going to keep her!" he exclaimed. Clearly the obvious answer, even though we had never had a house dog in twenty-one years of marriage, and we already had three outdoor dogs.

No matter—we adopted little orphan Annie.

The decision transformed my life. I doted on her. She went to the office with me on weekdays, curling up happily in a little bed next to my desk. We added her name to the masthead of the magazine, under the title "Staff (Moral) Support."

In my editorial, I said Annie's duties as chief of morale were small but significant.

"She goes from desk to desk throughout the day, wiggling her tail in approval of everyone's work and accepting the occasional pat on the head. She's passed her probation with flying colors and looks forward to a long, productive career here at the magazine. Welcome aboard, little Annie!"

Flying colors, indeed. She brightened our existence, at work and at home. Hank was coaching high school basketball at the time, and when we would come home at night after a game, Annie would turn herself inside-out to greet us at the door, all the while emitting soft, high-pitched whimpers of joy that were utterly endearing.

Annie was my hedge against loneliness. We were childless then, and not by choice. When Hank was away at basketball practice, the house could feel awfully empty. But not with Annie! She dogged my heels from room to room, snuggled next to me on the sofa, went out with me and the other dogs on walks and runs.

She did have her own ideas about certain things. In the car, she insisted on riding above the back seat, up next to the rear windshield. I said okay to that. At night, she indicated her sleeping preference by diving under the covers and worming her way to the bottom of our bed.

I demurred, placing a cozy pet igloo on the floor next to my side of the bed and suggesting we would both be more comfy if she slept there. Obligingly, she agreed.

In April, just two months after Annie had come to live with us, I learned something that astonished me. I had been having odd symptoms, the combination of which, under normal circumstances, might have led me to believe I was pregnant.

But Hank and I had been trying to conceive for eleven years by that time, with no success. We had endured most of what modern medical technology has to offer infertile couples, up to and including one round of in-vitro fertilization, all to no avail.

Yet, there it was. A positive result on a home pregnancy test kit. Soon after, a positive blood test. And then, mind-bogglingly, the affirmation from my gynecologist, who declared, after examining me, "Oh, yes! You're pregnant, all right."

Stunned, I went back and checked my calendar. What I saw gave me goose bumps. I had conceived *on the very first cycle after Annie came to us.*

Annie was the stork in disguise!

You hear stories about couples adopting a baby and then conceiving one, but...after adopting a dog?

Maybe. Maybe it can work that way when the adoptee is a little hard-luck creature that brings maternal instincts to the fore. We'll never know for sure.

What I do know is that Annie became as good a dog for a small child as she had been for a childless couple. Sophie was enchanted by her. "Addn" (the baby's approximation of "Annie") was almost her first word—second only to "Dadn."

And when Sophie got to the age where dressing up toys and dolls is *the* activity of choice, Annie allowed herself to be gently dressed up, too. (I have pictures to prove it.)

Annie was with us the rest of her life. When she departed, I knew I would want another dog like her someday, and eventually we acquired Sadie, a Pomeranian/Chihuahua cross.

Sadie was a hedge against the time when our daughter would head off to college. That's when our home would once again feel empty, and a small, special dog would be just what's needed to fill it up.

Chapter 8: Rest in Peace, Sweet Mare

It was just a kink in the uppermost branch of a gray pine tree, but it brought me up short. The pine stands over the grave of a special horse, and the reason the kink shocked me is the core of an unusual tale.

Tigress, my first horse, came into my life exactly when I needed her. I was a shy, intense thirteen-year-old, the proverbial ugly duckling. She was a green-broke Thoroughbred filly, to my young eyes ravishingly beautiful. With her, who cared if I never went out on a date, never had a boyfriend, never got married—all distinct possibilities to me at the time. I had Tigress!

Mostly a self-taught equestrian at that point, I could easily have run into trouble with her. Fortunately, Tigress was so forgiving, it didn't matter. She put up with me while I figured things out. She was timid, but willing and honest. She never said no to me out of defiance, orneriness, or guile. She sometimes said *I can't* out of fear or confusion, but never *I won't* or *You can't make me.*

Still, her timidity could be exasperating. Once, a friend and I hauled her to a local hunter/jumper show in a two-horse trailer with no divider. At the show, with strange sounds and smells to excite and intimidate her, Tigress decided not to back out of the trailer. Who knew what might lurk back there, waiting for her as she stepped blindly in reverse? Better to just stand her ground, or—*hey! Look! I can just turn right around, like this!*

Around she squeezed, her long Thoroughbred body bulging out the sides of the older wooden trailer. Then out she popped, her expression saying, "See? Much safer this way." My friend Teresa, a knowledgeable horse person, was appalled.

Yet Tigress could be brave when it mattered. A year or so after the trailer episode, as houses began to spring up around our rural neighborhood, I was dismayed when a new neighbor's pasture cut off our usual trail up the hillside. His fence was three-rail wood board, painted white, just under four feet high. One day, I was cantering Tigress along the path that led to the old trail, thinking with annoyance that we would soon have to stop.

But then, on a whim, I decided *not* to stop. As we approached the fence, I simply sat deeper and closed my legs around her. Tigress, pleased with this turn of events, sprang over the fence into our neighbor's field. We cantered the path as it led across the pasture, then bounded right over the fence on the other side, continuing up the hill at a gallop.

Never had I felt such exhilaration! Tigress and I were masters of the universe: bold, determined, unstoppable. We could go anywhere, do anything.

It was a glorious feeling for a fifteen-year-old girl.

Tigress remained mine as I transitioned into adulthood. And, when my husband and I eventually moved onto our own twenty acres, Tigress came with us.

Then, one chilly February morning years later, when Tigress was twenty-five, I found her on the ground, colicking. The veterinarian diagnosed an enterolith, a mineral-based stone growing in her gut and now blocking her colon. He administered mineral oil and a painkiller, and told me to keep her moving.

Not thinking clearly, I led her out onto the dirt road that borders our acreage, when I should have stayed closer to home. After about an eighth of a mile, she simply stopped and would go no farther, forward or back. She knew more than I did, perhaps more even than the vet.

I left her there and sprinted back to the house to summon the vet again. As I implored him to return at once, I could see her standing patiently, way out on the road, wearing her blue blanket.

When the vet arrived, I made that difficult decision, the one every animal lover dreads. I didn't want to put her through surgery at her age, so I agreed to let the vet put her down.

After he had left, I walked back to the house, stepped inside, and doubled over, keening a grief sharper than any I had felt in my life to that point. I think I was grieving for my lost childhood as much as for my sweet mare. Tigress had been my living, breathing link to those happy years. She had helped me to find myself; now, she was gone.

I found a backhoe driver willing to come that same day, retrieve her from the road, and bury her on our property. As he lowered her into the grave, her head dangled at an odd angle. I wanted to ask him to let me straighten out the kink in her neck, but I knew he was in a hurry—he was doing me a huge favor as it was. Plus, I knew it didn't really matter, anyway: her essence was gone.

Still, the thought of her positioned awkwardly continued to bother me. I finally consoled myself with the thought that I would plant a tree over the spot where her head now lay, and the roots of the tree would reach down and somehow (thinking in that odd way we sometimes do in times of extreme grief) make everything okay.

By the time spring arrived that year, there was indeed a tree growing on that spot. But I hadn't planted it. It was a native gray pine, volunteering its services for this duty.

Twenty years later, the pine's trunk measured about eight inches in diameter, almost large enough to support the commemorative plaque I planned to place on it. And when I glanced to the top of the tree that day, there was that kink. *The* kink, now removed from my mare and held aloft in the tree.

Or so it seemed to me, in that odd way of thinking that now reassures me my Tigress is truly resting in peace.

Part II. Leo & Locket: Cat Tales

I have lived with several Zen masters—all of them cats.
~ Eckhart Tolle

The feline friends gracing my life have taught me to look at the world with greater appreciation. Cats, like other animals, live in the moment, but they seem to specialize in getting the most out of that moment and its particulars. The warm pleasure of a patch of sunshine. The companionship of being near, but separate. The wonder of looking at nature with wide-open eyes.

To me, cats themselves are mini-miracles. Nowadays, people fawn over the latest miniaturized technical gadgets, from phones to laptops and tablets to gizmos I don't even know the names for. But to me, nothing is as remarkable as having, for your very own, a living, breathing creature every bit as wonderful as a cougar or tiger, only small and domesticated.

That is the house cat. I sing its praises!

Chapter 9: Jungle Cat

I've often wondered why anyone would want to keep a wild, exotic cat as a pet. Apart from the usual reasons why this is a bad idea (the cat can hurt you, you can inadvertently hurt the cat, it's illegal), there's the underappreciated fact that plain old house cats are near-perfect replicas of their wild cousins, only in miniature.

Why, then, have a hand-raised bobcat destroying the furniture when a common tabby will give you as much "bobcat" as you need, safely and inexpensively, while leaving (most) of your belongings intact?

More so than dogs, domestic cats resemble their wild forebears in every way. In fact, if you're not careful, they can wander off and start living on their own, like teenagers gone bad. Difficult-to-control feral cat populations attest to this.

Both my cats, Leo and Locket, are neutered and stick close to home. This reassures my husband and me, plus gives us ample opportunity to notice how much they remind us of wild cats— in their case, black panthers.

Leo, the brawny male, looks the most like a miniature panther, but Locket, his petite sister (nickname "Skinny Minnie" or "Min" for short) actually behaves more like one. This became especially obvious once Min discovered her "jungle." That's what

Hank and I call the small strip of green grass she's claimed as her own. It's just outside our front door, on the other side of the driveway, at the foot of a slope where there's a shallow trough. Wild grass grows well there, where water drains off the hill.

One especially rainy spring, the grassy patch grew luxuriant—seven inches and counting. The first time I noticed Min there, she was just sitting, peering out between the blades, her green eyes intent. A jungle predator, scouting her prey.

The next time I saw her in the same spot, I alerted my husband. We both watched as she hunkered down, flattening her ears and coiling her muscles, rocking back and forth almost imperceptibly to get just the right purchase. Her fierce eyes blazed, and you could sense the wheels of her imagination turning.

"Ah! An injured wildebeest!"

Then *whomp!* She pounced, capturing nothing in her paws but sheer joy. Then she paused, as if conjuring up a new victim, before whirling about and pouncing back to the original spot.

You cannot buy entertainment like this.

Once, when it was still damp and breezy from a recent rainstorm, I stepped out of the house to feed the barn animals, not at all expecting to see the cats outside in that weather. But there was Min, leaping about happily in her little jungle, undeterred by the wet grass, invigorated by the gusty wind.

Another time, I watched as her big brother, in an I'm-the-boss mood, chased her away from the grassy spot and triumphantly took her place. There he sat, regally—the new king of the jungle.

It's not all action, though. Sometimes Min just relaxes there, gazing about or munching daintily on a grass tip, thinking her secret cat thoughts.

I've learned a lot by watching her. She teaches me how to enjoy and value the smallest parts of nature. It's easy to be awed by mountains and rivers and glistening lakes and huge redwoods that tower far above your head. But there's equal glory in the humbler elements, if you take the time and effort to appreciate them. A squat pine tree, a spiky manzanita bush, even a plain old patch of grass...each can be as glorious in its own way as a full-blown tropical jungle.

Just ask my cat.

Chapter 10: Personality Plus

Darkness falls. Time to put our cats, Leo and Locket, into the garage for the night. "Leooo!" I call. "Locket!"

Leo bounds down from the hillside where he's been stalking gophers. I scoop him up. He purrs a greeting, glad to see me and happy to be taken into custody. I plunk him into the garage and close the door, then turn to the trickier task of catching his sister.

Locket will come when I call—sometimes—but then she turns coy. When I approach, she darts away, keeping just far enough ahead of me to elude capture. If I bide my time as long as it takes, she'll eventually surrender, sprawling luxuriantly in the driveway, inviting me to pick her up. When I do, she'll utter a quick meow, not a greeting as much as a declaration of her small but important presence.

This is but one of about a zillion ways my two cats differ from each other. Though as closely related as creatures can be without being identical twins, they each have distinct personalities, with their own quirks, behaviors, and mannerisms.

You know what I'm talking about. Your own pets, be they cats, dogs, birds—even gerbils—have their own unique traits and characteristics. Those of you with lizards and turtles will say they have identifiable personalities, too.

Amazingly, scientists have been slow to warm to the idea that animals have personalities. Until recently, most were reluctant to ascribe any personality traits at all to animals. Doing so seemed too close to anthropomorphism—that much-dreaded projecting of human characteristics on non-human entities. Scientists hate it.

Earlier experts even denied creatures sentience, much less personality. René Descartes, the seventeenth-century French philosopher, believed animals were mindless machines that could neither think nor feel pain. The work of the Russian Ivan Pavlov in the nineteenth century and American B. F. Skinner in the early twentieth century portrayed animals as merely reacting reflexively to their environment, or behaving only in response to positive or negative reinforcement. And as for personalities? No way.

In fact, it wasn't until as late as 1993 that a major psychology journal even published a paper applying the term *personality* to animals. In that study, Canadian researchers Roland Anderson and Jennifer Mather discovered distinct personality traits among, of all creatures, red octopuses. In their later work with giant Pacific octopuses, the pair found tons of personality—enough to give their tentacled subjects quirky names.

There was Emily Dickinson, a shy female prone to hiding behind her tank's rock outcroppings. And Lucretia McEvil, a lady octopus with a penchant for tearing apart her tank at night. And Leisure Suit Larry, a male unusually aggressive in the pursuit of, um, companionship.

In the years since Anderson and Mather's groundbreaking first study, a new field of animal personality has emerged. Researchers working within it are proving scientifically what animal lovers have known all along—that humans share behavior traits with a wide range of animals.

If this weren't true, it would be fruitless to use animals to test drugs for emotional and psychiatric disorders affecting humans. Yet we do use animals for this purpose, and it works—only because animals experience many of the same emotional states we do.

Indeed, today it's generally accepted that animals do indeed experience primary emotions at least—such as fear, anger, rage, surprise, joy, and disgust. Now the controversy swirls around whether they can have secondary emotions, as well. Secondary emotions—such as embarrassment, shame, guilt, and jealousy— are more complicated and tend to arise less rapidly.

The field of animal personality is booming, but there continue to be skeptics who insist that anthropomorphism remains at the root of it all--owners merely projecting their own personalities onto their animals. But as research continues to reveal more and more about animal emotions and cognition, these long-held opinions may soften.

In the meantime, animal lovers have their own opinions about the skeptics. Clearly, these people have never owned pets—and certainly never a cat.

Chapter 11: Garage-Door Terror

I t was a waking nightmare.

I had just hit the "close" button on the garage-door control panel and was climbing my front steps, arms full of shopping bags. From the corner of my eye, I glimpsed my sweet Leo, the feline love of my life, lying on the garage floor, directly in the path of the down-coming metal door.

"Leo! Move!" I shouted, stamping my feet and flapping my elbows in his direction. In classic cat fashion, he blinked and waved his tail languidly. The door appeared to be headed directly for his neck.

"*Leo!*" I shrieked. I didn't have the door's remote control on me, and there wasn't time to race back to the control panel on the garage wall. Half my brain was reassuring me the cat would jump away in the nick of time, as he and his sister generally did. But the other half was visualizing a kitty beheading.

Down came the door. There lay the cat. Before my eyes, the door landed smack on his neck, pinning him to the floor. Pitching my packages, I lunged for the control panel, slamming the "open" button. As the door started back up, Leo leaped to his feet, shook his head several times in astonishment, then bounded out of the garage and around the corner of the house.

That he moved at all somewhat reassured me, but I needed more than *that*. I followed him around to the backyard, fearing he would already be hidden somewhere under the deck where I couldn't reach him, in the manner of cats preparing (stoically) to die.

Instead, I found him in the garden, casually chewing on a plant stem. I lifted him gingerly and probed his neck for signs of heat, swelling, or tenderness. There was none. Responding to what felt to him like TLC, Leo began to purr. Even this didn't allay my fear, as I knew cats sometimes purr out of distress.

I placed him in the house and returned to the garage to measure the closed door's clearance from the floor—a sickening half-inch. The device's safety mechanism, which ordinarily reverses the door's action if it hits something solid, hadn't kicked in because Leo's neck didn't offer enough resistance.

For the cat, it must have seemed the equivalent of being throttled roughly for a moment, then let go. Not unlike being played with by small children.

Yet still I worried. What if the swelling was just starting now, and would eventually choke off his breathing? What if incipient damage to his spine would ultimately result in paralysis or who-knew-what? What if even now he lay unconscious in the house...?

I grabbed my packages and rushed inside, where I found Leo...doing fine. The rest of the afternoon, I kept him by my side and watched him carefully—no mean feat with a cat. He was fine.

When my daughter came home from school, we both watched him. Still fine. Toward evening, I began to appreciate the notion of cats' nine lives. I didn't know how many of Leo's lives were on the books before that morning (he and his sister had been rescued from a dumpster before my family adopted them as young adults), but I was sure he now had one fewer remaining.

And here's the point of the story. Pet owners often worry about their four-legged charges almost as much as they do their children, sometimes even regarding their animals as their "other children." I find this to be true even for larger pets, such as, in my family's case, goats and horses. I'm my gelding's "mom." I'm my daughter's pony's "grammy." My equestrian friends and acquaintances all refer to their horses (and their cats and dogs) as their "kids."

Is this weird, or just natural?

Either way, it makes pet-parenting about as anxiety-producing as genuine parenting. On the upside, it gives children a much truer taste of parenting than playing with dolls does. During her childhood, Sophie bottle-fed an infant orphan kitten, tended the bite-wounds of a young goat, oversaw the feeding program of her chubby pony, learned how to potty-train a puppy—all skills that will come in handy someday when she's a mom to a human baby.

As I ponder all this at my keyboard, Leo materializes at my side, announcing himself with a musical trill. It climbs in pitch, then hangs in the air, a sort of purred question mark. He wants into my lap.

"No, Leo. Mommy's working." He sits back and regards me with a disapproving look, then turns and springs effortlessly onto the messy table in back of me. Picking his way through the clutter, he heads for the bed I've made for him there—a wire in-basket lined with an old wool saddle pad.

He's safe for the moment, so I can relax. Except...where's his sister? Outside? If so, is she safe from roving dogs? Coyotes? Rattlesnakes? The UPS truck?

With pets, as with children, the worry never ends. I turn again and look at Leo in his comfy crib. He stares back at me, lowering his lids halfway and lifting his chin just a hair, adoring me with his expression.

No, the worry never ends. But neither, I realize gratefully, does the sweetness.

Chapter 12: Driven to Distraction

Our four-legged friends sometimes bring out our silly sides, and that's a good thing. I'm all for it—generally. But when it comes to automobile safety, silly doesn't make sense. The car is *not* a toy, no matter what my cat Leo may think. Even if I taught him to think that way.

Here's how it happened.

I was on my way to pick up my daughter from school and deliver her to her basketball game. Our longish driveway connects to our homeowners' association paved road which, once you turn onto it, angles downhill for a bit before heading back up.

From our house, our driveway meanders past our barn on the way to the association road. I always glance over to see whether the horses are at the barn as I drive by. Not sure why I do this, but I do. So my speed on this particular day, as on most days, was slow, giving me a chance to crane my neck toward the mare and gelding we owned at the time. Still, I was probably going a good ten miles per hour. I slowed slightly as I came to the end of our driveway to check for traffic, then pulled out and cruised on down the slope.

I reached the bottom of the hill, then accelerated on the incline and was about halfway up it when I heard a curious, soft-yet-substantial *whump* on the back of my car.

Whatever could cause such a sound? I checked my rearview mirror, and there, perched precariously on the trunk lid, leaning his black fur into the back windshield, hanging on for dear life, was...my cat, Leo.

What?

I pulled over and stopped the car, hopped out, and swept him into my arms, laughing and swearing and trying to reassure him, all at once.

"Poor kitty!" I crooned. "Did you wonder where you were going?" That's *all* I needed—to drive my cat off into unfamiliar territory, where he would wander off and get lost. Or hit by a car! (Or run over by my own car, for Pete's sake.)

I put him on the passenger seat and slipped back in behind the wheel. For the first time I could remember, this ordinarily unflappable creature seemed completely undone. As I turned the car around and headed for home, he crawled over onto my lap, trembling and purring out of stress.

"Poor kitty!" I told him, again and again, as he gripped my legs. "Brave kitty! Most courageous of kitties."

Surely you're wondering how I entered my car in the first place without noticing a cat on the roof. Well, Leo wasn't on the roof when I got into the car, in the garage. But, as I started the ignition, I did hear the characteristic *thud* of a cat jumping from the overhead storage area onto the car's roof, taking advantage of this handy "step stool" before it drove away.

This happens a lot. But it's generally the strategy of Locket, Leo's sister. *She's* the one who loves to hang out in that secretive overhead hideaway. She always hops right down from the car to the ground, however, and that's what I assumed happened on this day.

Bad assumption.

You may also wonder why Leo would stay up on the roof of a moving car, rather than also hopping down straightaway. After all, I have to back out and turn around, so there was plenty of time for him to do so.

And the answer to that question is, *I taught him to ride up on the car.*

Here's how *that* happened. Whenever my daughter and I come home from errands around suppertime, we stop at the barn to feed the horses before going on to the house. Saves a trip back out.

And sometimes, as we're finishing up at the barn, Leo will stroll out to greet us, happy that we're home. A few times, when he's come out he's hopped up onto the car, and we've let him stay there as I drive, v-e-r-y slowly, the remaining hundred yards or so up to the house.

When I say *we*, I really mean *I*, because it was I—the adult—who said, "Let's give Leo a ride!" And, that very first time, it was I who slid off the cover of the moon roof, so we could see Leo's flattened underside directly above us as we inched our way to the garage.

And it was I who said, "Wheeee! I'm king of the world!" on Leo's behalf. In my defense, I can only say that Leo did seem to enjoy it. When we arrived at the house, he hopped down and looked up at us as if to say, "Cool."

So, in essence, I had specifically *taught* him to ride on the top of the car. As if the car were a great big cat toy. How's that for modeling the behavior you want from your soon-to-be-driving teen?

Come to think of it, as I was backing and turning on the day of the unauthorized ride, I'm amazed I didn't fling him off the car myself. As I say, I was hurrying. I can just imagine Leo up there, clinging desperately with all four paws.

Boy, this isn't like the other rides! he must have been thinking.

As for me, when I taught him this clever trick, who knows what I was thinking. *Not* thinking, obviously. After the incident, I told Leo how smart he had been to hang on for dear life. And I told myself I had darned well better show some smarts, too—at least as much as my intelligent cat.

Chapter 13: Ferocious Felines

I looked at my two cats curled up together, dozing. Locket, aka Min for her diminutive size, made a small sound, a cross between a tiny mew and a purr. The other responded by tenderly washing his sister's ear. They were the picture of love and gentleness.

How jarring, then, to recall that just that morning I had found them torturing a baby mouse to death. The tiny creature, no bigger than my thumb, sounded exactly like a cat's squeaky toy, only at a higher, more desperate pitch. Whenever the mouse ran, both cats leapt after it eagerly, one of them eventually blocking its path or stepping on it with a paw to stop its frantic trajectory. Whenever it did stop, frozen in place but for the trip-hammering of its heart, the cats simply watched it, and waited.

Sometimes, bored and eager to resume the chase, they would taunt the mouse by leaning in close with their rapt faces, or slapping it with a paw.

What horrifies me most about these scenarios (which aren't uncommon in our decades-old rural home) is the blasé-yet-brutal manner of my otherwise sweet-tempered housecats. Whenever the mouse remains still, they're perfectly relaxed, glancing about and waving their tails lazily as if they're just kicking back, doing nothing.

But the instant the mouse so much as flicks a whisker, their eyes and ears relock onto it with deadly intent. If it tries to scurry away, they chase with murderous glee. Only if the mouse comes close to getting away will one of the cats actually grasp it in his or her jaws and carry it to another, more contained spot, where it will be put down to resume its terrifying ordeal.

Once, Min, presumably when she wanted a rest, crouched down on top of the mouse, trapping it under her breast. Imagine the mouse's confused, suffocating panic at that point, smothered in this faux maternal embrace.

Left unchecked, this persecution will continue until the mouse dies of tiny fang-punctures, or perhaps is literally frightened to death. Later, I'll find the tiny corpse, limp and moist with cat spit.

Whenever I'm there to witness it, however, I intervene. I have a small, lidless shoebox I use for this purpose. I follow the darting trio and try to trap the mouse under the box.

This is even more difficult than it sounds. The mouse doesn't know I'm trying to save it, of course; it's as terrified of me as it is of the cats. Locket and Leo, meanwhile, keep getting in my way, making a clean catch next to impossible. If daughter Sophie is at home, the scene is punctuated with her anxious shrieks— she's both afraid of the mouse and concerned for its safety.

If I manage to catch the mouse, I slide a piece of cardboard under the box and carry it outside. If the mouse is too quick for me, I have another, lidded shoebox, into which I've cut a mouse hole at one bottom corner. I place this box along the wall where the cats are taunting the mouse, and wait for the mouse to run into the hole. Then I cover the hole and carry the box out.

The irony here, of course, is that we routinely set mouse traps whenever we suspect a mouse is about. I refuse to coexist with rodents, and have no qualms about their being instantly snapped to death in a trap.

But allowing any creature, even a rodent, to be tortured to death is another matter. Once rescued, of course, the mouse becomes my ward and is granted permanent immunity. It's no longer "a mouse"; it's "the mouse we rescued." A refugee mouse. It cannot be killed.

That means Sophie and I must carry it as far from the house as we can, then set it loose to recover and make a new life for itself—away from us, we hope.

Once, we carried a mouse several hundred yards, crossing the nearest road, and set the creature free in a field adjoining our property. The mouse took a moment to orient itself, then scurried back across the road, making a beeline in the direction of our house. Without our cats' expert help, we couldn't catch the tiny creature again. I told myself it found a more appealing home in the brush long before it reached our house, but I'm not at all sure of that.

Mother Nature can be cruel; there's no denying it. But the cats themselves aren't cruel. They're simply doing what nature has programmed into them. I wish it didn't have to be this way. I wish baby animals didn't have to be tormented by other animals. I wish no creatures, animal or human, had to suffer in the ways they often do. That such suffering is a fact of life on our planet makes Mother Nature darn hard to understand.

Chapter 14: Problem Child

O ne of my most challenging cat problems occurred when my daughter went off to college. The feline in question was willowy little Locket, who belongs mostly to Sophie. (Locket's litter-mate, Leo, is more mine.) And when "her" human departed for higher learning, little Locket—also known as Skinny Minnie or Min—became a problem child.

We bring our cats in at night to protect them from predators. They sleep in the garage, or in the one bathroom they have nighttime access to through a kitty door from the garage. When it's time, Leo usually comes to my call. He's easy to get in. Min is another matter. She's coy.

Because Min loves my daughter, Sophie is generally able to lure her in with a beseeching, melodious call she developed just for this purpose.

"Where's my Min? Awwww, Min! Where's my pretty kitty? Come on in, beautiful cat! Minnie-Min-Min-Min...." And so on. Sophie delivers it in a honeyed lilt, which makes me roll my eyes. It shouldn't, though, because it works.

With Sophie gone, corralling Min at night has become my job, and I'm terrible at it. At first I tried putting out my usual call. Leo would run in, but Min would linger, just out of reach. I would back away from the door, trying to draw her in by "creating space." She would pad up to the threshold, then pause, switching her tail. (And smirking. I'm sure of it.) If I took the tiniest step toward her, she would skitter back into the darkness of the night.

Finally, it occurred to me to mimic Sophie's call. So, rolling my eyes, I tried it. And it worked! Exactly once. Min heard the teasing, pleading call and came bounding. Once inside, though, her disappointment—then disdain—were palpable.

"Oh, it's *you*? Not Sophie?" I snatched her up that time, but the copycat call never worked again. Instead, I had to resort to luring her with milk, which our kitties ordinarily don't get because vets tell us cats don't digest lactose well. But we didn't have any cream (much less lactose), and this was a matter of some urgency.

My strategy was to bring the jug to the door and slosh the milk around as noisily as possible. This would bring Min trotting in with her nose in the air. I would usher her into the special bathroom along with Leo, and pour just a lap or two of milk into her bowl.

Sophie had cautioned me against this. "You'll spoil her," she said. "Plus milk makes her vomit." It's maddening when your kid is smarter than you. Min did in fact begin spitting up even this tiny bit of milk. By then she was, in fact, spoiled, and I had to find something else to bribe her with. I wound up buying special cat food, the multiflavored kind in the teensy cans. Expensive, but it works. I dole it out in thimble-size amounts.

Though I love all my animals equally, Min still seems affection-starved with Sophie gone. This causes me feelings of guilt. While Sophie was still home, Min would sit next to her on the sofa as my daughter read or worked on her laptop. Sophie would croon to the cat from time to time and stroke her silky coat.

I *would* do all this for Min, except the spot next to me is already taken. When I'm enjoying a coffee break and a magazine, Sadie, our Pomeranian/Chihuahua cross, nestles next to me as I sit in my favorite chair. If Min (or Leo) so much as looks my way, she growls a warning that's surprisingly menacing for a dog so small.

(Yes, this is aggressive behavior, and she's not supposed to do it, but she was sixty-something in human years at that point and not likely to change.)

Min persists, in spite of the growl. My chair is mission style, with flat, wooden arms. One time, Min circled to the back, then jumped up on the chair's arm so she was just above and behind where Sadie was resting next to me. The dog whirled about and "rattlesnaked" (the term describes the high-pitched snarl), blasting the cat back down.

Undaunted, Min circled to the other side, hopped up on the sofa next to the chair, then hurtled herself over the coffee cup on that arm of the chair and into my lap.

Chaos ensued. Sadie rattlesnaked Min down again—more viciously this time—and I couldn't even scold her because I was too busy searching for cat hair in my coffee cup. But can you ever be sure, really, one tiny little hair hasn't slipped in?

You cannot. My break ruined, I stumped to the kitchen and dumped the remaining coffee down the drain.

This is not how I envisioned my golden years. My husband and I have just the one child, so we've never had to deal with sibling rivalry. Now, though, with all my four-legged "children," I've got it in spades.

I'll keep trying to solve my animal problems as best I can. But feeling guilty and inadequate all the time? That I'll just have to live with.

Part III. Zest for Life: Sadie Dog

Heaven goes by favor. If it went by merit,
you would stay out and your dog would go in.
~Mark Twain

I have a life coach. She's wonderful, and she covers all of life's most important principles. She teaches by example, which is by far the best way to teach. And her lessons are simple.

Love unconditionally. Forgive immediately. Show gratitude continuously. Don't judge.

Greet each day with exuberance. Do what you enjoy. Honor your routines. Sleep well.

Be loyal. Be agreeable. And when necessary, stand your ground.

You may've guessed by now that my coach is a dog. Her species is known as our "best friend," though "best counselor" might be more to the point.

I'm still learning from my little dog, Sadie. Her full name, as given by my then-young daughter years ago, is Sadie Suebear Sweetheart.

As you'll see, the name fits.

Chapter 15: Puppy Love

Peer people fall into categories. There are morning people and night people. Detail people and big-picture types. Active folks and couch potatoes.

Dog people and cat people.

True dog lovers find dogs friendly and agreeable, while cats seem fussy and dismissive. Cat lovers find cats interesting and complicated, like a fine wine, while dogs seem fawning and over-the-top.

Cat people think other cat lovers are cerebral; dog people think other dog lovers are down-to-earth.

I've always assumed I was in the cat camp. I've owned cats (or been owned by them) most of my life. When my family acquired our two current cats, coal-black littermates Leo and Locket, they ruled supreme in our dog-free household. Then everything changed.

It began one spring, when my husband, daughter, and I attended a family gathering at the home of my sister's mother-in-law, Pat. That's when we met Pat's then four-month-old puppy, Zelda.

It was adoration at first sight.

Of course, all puppies are irresistible. What my family and I felt for this little dog, however, went beyond the predictable attraction. Zelda was pint-sized—only about four pounds—and resembled no discernable breed. In fact, she was a Pomeranian/Chihuahua cross, yet she looked for all the world like a mutt, with floppy ears, a "smiling" face, and a spotted caramel-and-white coat. Only *tiny*.

Zelda's energy seemed inversely related to her size. She zoomed around the house, everyone's playmate, an inexhaustible source of pure entertainment. Then, all at once, she would run out of gas and fall asleep, curled up in her little bed or on your shoulder—she didn't care which.

Before the day was over, though there had been no prior discussion about getting a dog, my family knew it needed a dog like Zelda. Actually, *needed* isn't a strong enough word. *Craved* is more like it. In mere hours, we had become addicted.

I asked Pat where she had found Zelda, and she gave me the name of the woman from whom she had acquired the dog. I called and discovered that Zelda's aunt, a Chihuahua, had just had a litter of two. The father was the same Pomeranian that had sired Zelda.

"We'll take one," I said, sight unseen.

We were gambling, of course. There's no guarantee that two animals, even when closely related, will be much like each other, especially in personality. But in all the ways that matter, our Sadie is a dead ringer for Zelda. She's tiny and cute. She's Miss Exuberance. And her mission in life is apparently to bring sheer joy into our household.

She's good at it, too.

Mind you, she doesn't look exactly like Zelda. She's lighter in color, with no white in her coat except for a smidge on each paw, one on her chest, and another on the tip of her tail. She also has a few white hairs on her forehead that look like a teensy, feathery heart.

The only thing big about Sadie are her eyes, which have that soulful, ringed-with-mascara look. If her ears were a bit longer, she would look just like the little Cocker Spaniel of *Lady and the Tramp* fame. If you hold her ears back, she looks like a baby harp seal, only russet.

When we first brought her home, at just under eight weeks of age, our two cats regarded her with keen interest. At that point, Sadie was smaller than many of the woodland creatures they had stalked and killed. Moreover, as a puppy, she appeared to them delightfully vulnerable.

They approached her stealthily, eyes bright. When they got close enough for a good whiff, however, they shrank back in alarm: "Yikes—it's a *dog!*"

Three months later, the cats began to have the same sort of exasperated tolerance for the puppy that young children have for even-younger siblings. At about five pounds, Sadie was then half the size of Leo, our black panther of a housecat. But that didn't stop her from mauling him.

At first, Leo would sit on his haunches, front paw raised in warning, and watch as Sadie circled him warily. Then they would begin to rough-and-tumble together. Leo would tolerate Sadie's bullying for a while, then eventually cuff her in an I-mean-business way. On these occasions, Sadie would retreat with a yip, then rebound with a vengeance, her intense, high-pitched growl sounding like a rattlesnake's warning.

Is Sadie more work than a cat? Yes, she is. Is housebreaking a laborious process, even using the crate method? Yes, it is. Is it fun to pick up the microscopic flecks of paper that result when she snatches a tissue out of the wastebasket and shreds it? No, it is not.

In truth, puppies are a lot of work—as are children, spouses, friendships, and most things in life worth having.

And as for dogs versus cats? I guess I can't say I'm a cat person anymore, in the sense that I prefer them to dogs. But neither do I think dogs are more appealing than cats, Sadie notwithstanding.

I guess you would have to call me an equal-opportunity animal lover.

Chapter 16: Sadie, Come Home

I t's astonishing how a creature so tiny can have such an enormous impact on a family.

We had left our little dog, Sadie, at the veterinarian's to recuperate after surgery that made sure she would never become a mom. She had been away only since the previous morning, yet my husband, daughter, and I kept bumping uncomfortably into the fact of her absence.

Sadie, our Pomeranian/Chihuahua cross, was then nine months old, which meant we were about three months late getting her spayed. The ideal time, vets tell us, is before the dog is six months old (the age at which they're likely to come into heat for the first time). And I had good intentions, honestly. At five months old, though, Sadie was still so tiny—about four-and-one-half pounds—that it was impossible to think of her on an operating table. When she was seven months old, I finally steeled myself and scheduled the appointment. Then, the day before "the day," she came into heat.

Technically, a dog can be spayed while she's in heat. Everyone I asked assured me there's only a slight additional risk of something going wrong. *Additional* risk? That wasn't going to work. I cancelled the appointment, bought a package of the tiniest doggie diapers I could find, and prepared to wait it out.

Have you ever seen a dog wearing a diaper? Even Sadie knew she looked ridiculous. Plus, they felt funny to her. When we set her back down after fitting her into her very first pair, she lifted one hind leg and held it in the air, the expression in her huge, beautiful eyes saying, "I can't move."

We cajoled and encouraged, and finally she put that hind leg down and raised the other, delicately, still gazing sorrowfully at my daughter, Sophie, and me. When she finally did attempt walking, it was in a slow succession of exaggerated, rolling high-steps, giving her the appearance of a tiny, bowlegged pirate.

You hate to laugh at an animal, especially one regarding you with mournful eyes. But it would have been humanly impossible not to. Eventually, Sadie returned to walking normally. Before long, she was scooting about, jumping on the sofa, and doing all the things she typically did, unmindful of her diaper.

While she was at the vet's, however, we missed all those antics, and even her bark. True to her small-dog heritage, she loves to bark. We were in the process of teaching her that three or four yaps (to announce the arrival of someone at the door or a feline transgression) was well and sufficient. Ten or twelve or a hundred barks, however, was overkill. And she was starting to get it, too, when I finally figured out how to convey the concept to her.

We had done it exactly wrong in the beginning. We would shout "Sadie! Stop barking!" whenever she went beyond the allotted number of yaps. Curiously, this didn't work. And her not-learning was odd, because we had easily taught her to sit, lie down, and stay.

It actually took me a quick "dog barking stop" online search to remind myself of something I should have remembered: that you teach an animal by rewarding the behavior you want, not by punishing—no matter how mildly—what you don't. (Positive reinforcement is how we housebroke her, of course, in addition to how we approached obedience training.)

So, we shifted to this strategy: When Sadie barked, we would immediately hold up a treat and say, in a low-yet-insistent voice, "Quiet dog! No bark!" Then, when she stopped barking (the sight of the treat distracted her, which enabled her to stop) and was quiet for five or six seconds (this part was harder, but she eventually began to understand), she got the treat.

When we first started with this method, we neglected the wait-five-or-six-seconds part. We were so delighted whenever the "shriek-barking" ceased, we handed over the reward instantly. Problem was, this highly intelligent creature soon turned the tables on us. She would run up, bark excitedly for no reason, then stop and look at us expectantly: "Where's my treat?" We were actually teaching her *to* bark.

But the addition of the momentary pause clarified for her that it was the cessation of barking we were after, not the barking itself.

Only with her gone, we actually missed the barking.

"It's so quiet," we kept saying to one another—"quiet" meaning drab, less joyful. And the other thing we kept saying was: "How did we ever live, before, without her?"

Fortunately, we didn't have to much longer. I picked her up later that day...armed with her favorite blankie and her favorite chew toy.

Plus plenty of stop-yapping treats.

Chapter 17: My Dog, Myself

May I someday be the person my dog thinks I am.
This popular adage expresses a worthy goal, if a challenging one. Your dog thinks you're the best, smartest, kindest person in the world. Endlessly interesting. One hundred percent benevolent. Never, ever wrong. When I think of how my little dog Sadie regards me, it makes me wince. To paraphrase Wayne and Garth, "I'm not worthy."

Dogs not only idolize us, they also embody everything we should strive for as decent human beings. Think of it. For starters, they wake up happy every day. I don't achieve that goal myself, but it's hard to be grumpy when there's an eight-pound ball of fur vibrating joyfully in front of you. Sadie wiggles about, then sits up on her haunches, tail still wagging. Then—and this is what slays me—while sitting up, she'll swipe her paws at her snout, one after the other, like a little prize fighter.

The message couldn't be clearer. Her body language says to everyone in the family, "Just seeing you *rocks my day!*" If you can't get your morning off on the right foot after a greeting like that, there may be no hope for you.

After my husband and daughter leave for work and school, Sadie gallops ahead of me down the hallway, ears pinned back for speed, the force of her trajectory indicating that this idea of mine—going to the home office—is excellent. Brilliant, even. Fantastic!

On the way downstairs, she stops briefly at her toy cache to grab a stuffed animal to bring along. (My office is a burial ground for dog toys and chew bones—they all wind up there, eventually.) Then she whizzes into the office, slams on the brakes, slings the toy onto the rug and looks up at me, delighted with herself and the day.

So, yes, dogs have *joie de vivre* to spare, every day, but that's just the beginning. Dogs also live their gratitude the way each of us knows we should. Like little Buddhists, they exist perfectly in the moment, thankful for everything that comes their way.

There's an old joke about a dog's diary that illustrates this point. "8 a.m., dog food. My favorite thing! 9:30 a.m., car ride. My favorite thing! 9:40, walk in the park. My favorite thing!" And so on right through the day. Completely accurate.

Dogs also strive to please us and to get along. Sadie believes barking is her heritage—her *raison d'être*. She's learned, however, that too much barking displeases her family, so she struggles to "keep it down."

I'll be at my computer, and I'll hear a muted, strangled sound behind me. I'll look around, and there will be Sadie on high alert, her gaze riveted out the window. It may be a deer that's strayed near the house. Or a turkey vulture that's cruised into our airspace. Or a squirrel with the audacity to come down out of his tree.

Whatever it is, Sadie will be locked onto the intruder and summoning the full force of her willpower NOT to bark. The result is that gurgling sound...a dog's version of *sotto voce*.

She tries so hard!

Dogs are also paragons of forgiveness. If you accidentally step on a paw, they'll shriek to high heaven, but then forgive you instantly—no retaliating, no whining, no sulking. "It's fine, really," they say. "Not a problem. Sorry I had my paw in that spot where your foot needed to be. My mistake."

And a dog's trust in us is absolute. Sadie puts her faith in me even when she knows it's time for a bath, or I'm about to pull a tick from her ear, or I'm wielding the scissors and need to give her the, um, hygiene clip.

"You want to trim hair from around *there*? OK...I *guess*. You'll be very, very careful?"

Patience is another sterling canine virtue. When I need to work, Sadie curls up like a church mouse in the small nest I've made for her next to my desk, biding her time. When we're getting ready to go for a walk, and I find one more thing to do before we go, then one more thing, then just one more...she waits quietly, patiently.

When the family is having dinner, she lies propped on her chest under the table, calmly gnawing a chew bone. When the clinking of silverware stops, she'll come to me tentatively, place her front paws on the edge of my chair, and gaze up into my face. "My turn yet?"

If I shake my head, she'll go back to her chew bone and work it a bit longer, then return politely to ask again.

Dogs struggle so hard to understand us! They strive to know what we're thinking, what we feel in our hearts. When I speak to her, Sadie tips her head from side to side in what almost seems a parody of attempted understanding. She wants so earnestly to "get" me, and most often, she does.

So, as the saying goes, I do hope someday to be the person she thinks I am. But I also want simply to be more like *her*.

Because she's not only my dog and a true friend. She's a role model.

Chapter 18: An Indelicate Matter

C an dogs get embarrassed? Animal behaviorists say no, arguing that embarrassment is a secondary emotion dogs aren't capable of. But sometimes, I wonder. And at one time in particular I could have sworn my little dog was blushing under her haircoat at something that had happened.

It was near bedtime, which is about 9 p.m. in the Meyer household. Husband Hank was already in bed, reading. Our daughter, Sophie, was in her bedroom doing homework. I was in the bathroom, brushing my teeth.

Now, ordinarily, Sadie would be on the bed with Hank at this moment, either snuggling at his feet or waggling her way up to his face to steal a kiss. After hanging with me all day, she uses the time just before lights-out to visit with her "dad" before going into Sophie's room, where she spends the night.

In fact, our little Pomeranian/Chihuahua cross knows the routine so well that as soon as I step out of the bathroom, she jumps down from our bed, trots down the hall and into Sophie's room, and hops up onto the foot of *that* bed.

On this particular night, however, Sadie wasn't where she normally would be. I sensed her presence in the bathroom and looked down. There she was, standing hesitantly, right behind me. The odd thing (apart from her being there as opposed to in her usual spot on our bed) was her demeanor.

Her large, brown eyes were troubled; her plume of a tail, drooping. She kept glancing away from me in a vague sort of way. It was as if she were attempting to attract my attention, yet regretted having to do so.

She seemed...well, embarrassed.

Then it hit me. As part of our nighttime routine, I take her outside for her final potty walk of the day. I had indeed taken her out on this night, and now I knew what was wrong.

I reached down and picked her up—carefully—and set her on the bathroom countertop. I gingerly lifted her tail and, sure enough, *there it was*...a petite-pea-size bit of leftover "business" clinging to her soft, gauzy haunch hair.

Mystery solved! No wonder she felt sheepish. In her indelicate condition, she sensed she was somehow "not OK." She also figured she had better stay off the bed. Knowing she needed help—and immediately—she came to the person she always turns to when things get gnarly. Me.

When we first got Sadie, she was to be Sophie's pet. But she's always been my dog, really. (When I was a child, I could never figure out why all our family dogs seemed to "belong" to my mother. Now I know. Mothers are the providers of all things good...food, comfort, squeaky toys.)

At seven or eight weeks old, Sadie was about the size of a soda can. While Hank was at work and Sophie at school all day, Sadie was with me while I wrote in my office. I would take her outside every hour without fail, and she would step about daintily on the pine needles, sniffing the ground, quickly picking up on the notion that being outside meant "go."

Our house and our yard were her entire universe. I was her supreme being...her guide to everything that mattered in her young life. So naturally she would turn to me now, upon finding herself in a grim and untidy predicament.

"I'm sorry," I told her. It was, in fact, my fault. I had been meaning to trim those cottony fanny hairs—I do it periodically to avoid exactly this problem. But I had procrastinated, and now she was suffering the awkward consequence.

"Not to worry," I assured her, then called to my daughter for help. Sophie gently steadied the dog while I held up her tail and snip-snipped away, thereby solving both the immediate and the ongoing problem.

Then my daughter went back to her homework; Sadie, her buoyancy restored, trotted off to visit with Hank; and I resumed my tooth-brushing, more amazed than ever at the intelligence and resourcefulness of our little dog.

Not to mention her ability to feel embarrassment.

Take that, you animal behaviorists.

Chapter 19: Naughty, Naughty Sadie

As it turns out, my good little dog, Sadie, is by some measures a delinquent. I didn't discover this until she was ten years old. The realization came as the result of a weekend trip my husband and I were planning to take. We normally place Sadie with a family member when we're away, or board her at the veterinarian's, where we know she's safe, secure, and well-cared-for—doted on, even.

This time, however, I came across a local ad for what looked like truly enlightened dog-sitting. It wasn't a kennel, where dogs are kept in separate cages. It was simply the home of genuine dog lovers, where the "guests" are treated the way they are at their own homes—like four-legged members of the family.

I'll call this place Dog's Delight, as that's what it sounded like to me. The dogs "on holiday" aren't separated from each other. Instead, they're allowed to frisk and play and hang out together, sort of like an extended stay at a dog park, only with meals and doggy beds provided.

Excited, I emailed Hank at work about this potential home-away-from-home option for our sensitive little dog.

"It sounds perfect!" I gushed. "And check these testimonials—'Best alternative to home our dogs have experienced.' And, 'The care and affection our dog received were second to none.' And, my favorite, 'When I came to pick him up, he didn't even want to leave.' How great is that? And it's less expensive than boarding her at the vet's."

I told my husband I would give Dog's Delight a call. Then, on second thought, I decided to check the fine print on the facility's website first. Under "Requirements," it said "guests" had to be at least eight months old, reliably housebroken, spayed or neutered, and up-to-date on vaccinations. Check, check, check, and check. So far, so good.

Then came the behavior requirements.

"Non-aggressive toward pets." Uh-oh. Does charging the cats count? Sadie is smaller than either Leo or Locket, our housecats, but she's been known to strike at them with a fierceness that would shame a viper. She never draws blood, but still.

"Non-aggressive towards people." Oh, dear. Does grabbing the bug-exterminator man's pant leg count? This happens when he comes to the door and I open it without remembering to pick Sadie up first.

"Non-protective of food or toys." Yikes. This one is a clear fail. Sadie is as protective of her things as a cranky mama bear is of her cubs.

Three strikes, and she's out. Clearly, our little dog wouldn't be a welcome guest at Dog's Delight. Though disappointed, I understood these rules completely. Obviously, the happy-dog-pack concept won't work unless every dog in the pack is other-dog friendly. And Sadie often isn't.

All this called to mind advice I've heard about how to choose a puppy to increase your odds of getting one with a friendly, submissive personality. You're supposed to pick up the puppy and hold it gently just behind its front legs, letting it hang down as you peer into its face. Does the puppy struggle to get away, or does it relax and let you hold it this way?

Similarly, turn the puppy on its back and cradle it like a baby in your arms, just for a moment. Does it seem comfortable and copacetic, or does it, again, struggle to get away? If you choose the pup that passes these handling tests, chances are you'll get one with the kind of temperament that generally gets along well with people and other dogs.

In other words, one that would always be welcome at a doggy sleepover.

I didn't know of this advice at the time I chose Sadie. She was one of just two pups in the litter, both female. Sadie was cuter and more confident, so that settled that. Had I picked her up and performed the tests, determined to select a submissive pup, I suspect she would have "failed" and I might have chosen her sister.

I'm glad I didn't.

Part IV. Our Noble Partners:
Horses & Ponies

God forbid that I should go to any heaven
in which there are no horses.
~ R.B. Cunningham Graham

Horses are living contradictions. They're powerful, yet gentle. Flighty, yet tractable. They look like works of art, yet are capable of doing the most strenuous work on our behalf. Yes, they have minds of their own, yet they're perfectly willing to carry us on their backs and do our bidding.

You can get as attached to a horse as you do to a dog or cat, but horses aren't just lovable companions. They also make possible many of our most cherished dreams—of competition and adventure and simple, unbounded freedom.

That's why horses and ponies fill a special niche in my canon of four-legged friends. They're our working partners, plus they inspire us to become better people…because only then can we become better horse trainers.

A part of my heart belongs to every horse or pony that's graced my life…including the ones you'll meet here.

Chapter 20: Sophie's Jewel

I was at my computer, working on an article. Struggling over the wording of a sticky paragraph, I heard a rap on my home-office door, the one that leads to the outside. It was the sound of a small pebble hitting glass. I opened the door and there, at the head of the driveway, stood my then nine-year-old daughter, Sophie, holding her pony.

Diamond's tail was done up in a sky-blue wrap. Her forelock, braided, decorated her face; her brushy Norwegian Fjord mane sparkled with gold glitter. Draped in the green-and-blue blanket Santa had brought for Christmas, Diamond looked like a pint-sized polo pony cooling out between chukkers.

Sophie, grinning happily, had just spent over an hour down at the barn, brushing, braiding, and dressing her pony. A riding lesson would come later in the day, but that wasn't the point of all this fuss and bother. This was purely for fun.

"How does she look?" Sophie asked. Eying the two of them, I thought of my own horse-filled childhood, remembering not the lessons or the shows, but all the time in between. Time spent out at the barn, by myself or with my sisters, messing with the horses. Not doing or learning anything specific. Just having fun.

I recalled the time our four horse-loving cousins came over, and we haltered one of our ponies and took him with us out on a walk. For the better part of a morning, we kids trudged up and down the countryside, winding through trees, stepping over tiny creeks, pretending to be a pioneer family on the move.

Another time, my two younger sisters and I rode our horses up the hill to a place where a long clearing in the trees suggested a wagon road from days gone by. We explored the length of this lost road, imagining the types of horse-drawn vehicles that might have used it. Ultimately, perhaps inevitably, we wound up racing up and down its winding length. During these short matches, my youngest sister's pony, Sherry, amazed us by keeping up with the two horses, Tigress and Showgirl.

We lived on 10 oak-covered acres, on which my father had built a tiny barn consisting of a tack-and-feed room and one stall. A whimsical artisan, he had added a short porch with a hand-tooled railing and an overhang in front, so that the structure resembled an old-fashioned country store.

I spent many happy moments inside that barn, including during springtime rainstorms. My sisters and I would laze about on the porch, under the overhang, with one or more horses or ponies tied to the hitching rail in front. Or we would be in the tack room, with a horse or two in the stall, all of us listening to the light rain singing on the barn's metal roof.

Though I had never shared this particular memory with Sophie, she, too, loved to be with her pony in the rain. In her preadolescence, she spent a lot of happy time with Diamond in the barn, or leading her around our brushy five-acre pasture.

One time, Sophie came into the house drenched from head to foot. I eyed her questioningly.

"What've you been up to?"

She described an afternoon spent with Diamond, out in the rain. She had built a makeshift enclosure for the pony in a far corner of the pasture, where pine trees and brush provide plenty of "building material."

Diamond had allowed herself to be contained like this for a while, corralled by dead brush and broken branches. Then, tiring of it, she had simply pushed her way through and gone back to the barn. By then, soaking wet and getting hungry, Sophie had headed back to the house.

It's easy to forget about this sort of fun when you're an adult. With so many entries on the perpetual to-do list, grown-ups are usually trying to make fun do double-duty. Hobbies are focused on lessons and learning new skills. Everything has a purpose, a goal to be achieved. It takes a child to remind us that just plain fun can be a goal, too. And a good one.

"Mom, how does she *look*?" The query, insistent this time, snapped me back to the present. "She looks grand," I said. Sophie turned and led her pony back to the barn, satisfied.

I returned to my computer, feeling oddly refreshed. The paragraph I had been wrestling with fell into place. I made a mental note, something to add to the to-do list, or perhaps to that list of words to live by.

To recharge batteries, hit the "play" button.

And if you can't remember how, ask a child.

Chapter 21: Growing Pains

I hadn't been thinking of buying a new pony. But the comment my daughter's riding instructor made that fateful day started the wheels in my head turning.

"Sophie looks bigger all of a sudden," Martin said, watching her trot around the arena on Diamond, her 12.2-hand Norwegian Fjord/Welsh Pony cross.

He wasn't wrong. Sophie *did* look almost too big for her little buckskin mare. I made a mental note to keep an eye peeled for something taller. That way, when the time did come to "level up," we might already know of some options and not have to rush.

With that in mind, I went to the online horse-buying resource that had led me to Diamond two years earlier. With a few casual clicks, I found a 14.1-hand grade pony, solid black and terribly cute. Shown extensively by children, he was reasonably priced and even located nearby. Couldn't hurt to look, I told myself.

Then, when the trainer led him out of the barn and handed him to Sophie to tack up, my interest quickened. The gelding regarded us with a friendly, dignified reserve. He was interested but not fawning, and extremely level-headed.

Sophie saddled him up, rode him around the arena, even popped him over a jump. A loopy grin never left her face. "He's fun-n-n-n!" she sang out, cantering him a few bonus laps. Clearly, she felt completely safe on his back.

By then, of course, we were well past the point of no return.

The pony's owners agreed to a one-week trial. He behaved beautifully during that time, impressing me, our riding instructor, and Sophie alike. Then he even won over the pre-purchase veterinarian, who pronounced our prospect both sane and sound.

So that explains how—before we could say, "Um, what about Diamond?"—the handsome gelding we came to call Brego became ours.

And what of Diamond? This was the pony that had helped my daughter learn to ride, carried her in her first little shows, and took her on adventures down to the river. The dilemma over what to do with the petite buckskin felt much like the mixed emotions parents feel when a child reaches a new milestone. Yes, we're thrilled our little one is now toddling, but oh! how we'll miss those darling rug-rat days. We don't want to give up any of it.

So it is with our children's mounts. Even when one is "sadly outgrown," it's hard to give up that trusty equine friend. From the child's perspective, of course, the solution is easy. Just keep the old horse as well as the new one. But the new horse will naturally get most of the riding, often leaving the other to languish.

Then, too, there's the question of hoarding. The kindly man who trimmed Diamond's feet for us scolded me when I mentioned the possibility of keeping her.

"Don't be selfish!" he chided, bending over Diamond's hoof. "Good ponies are hard to find. She should go on to be some other kid's horse, not stand around in your pasture while your daughter rides her new pony."

He had a point. Then again, Diamond was aging. Though she had many years of service left to give, I wanted to be able to know she would be well cared for when her time came to retire.

In the end, a good friend of mine unwittingly helped me decide. Then mentoring a young girl, Sue asked whether she could bring the seven-year-old over for rides on Diamond. Absolutely, I told her. In that moment, I realized there would probably be opportunities for me to lease or loan Diamond to other young riders, as well, giving them the benefit of her wisdom while allowing me to retain control of her future.

A perfect solution! Except, of course, for the precedent it set.

"These aren't Breyer horses," I reminded my daughter. "You can't collect them forever." Sophie said she understood.

I just hoped we both would remember this caveat the next time growing pains sent us looking for a new four-legged friend.

Chapter 22: My Equine Advisor

It was a watershed moment. I had been thinking out loud, mulling over my next move with the part-warmblood gelding I had bought for myself the year before. Killian's Red, a tall, handsome chestnut, was supposed to be my "packer" over jumps. I was taking lessons with my daughter's instructor, jazzed about learning to jump again now that Sophie was in Pony Club. But in that way that often happens with horses, Killian was turning out to be more complicated than expected, and it was unnerving me.

Driving to the feed store on a Saturday morning, I thought it through.

"Maybe with the tuning up he's getting now, it'll work out," I said to my daughter, sitting beside me. "So far, he doesn't feel that different to me, but I know I need to give it more time."

Sophie turned to me, an earnest look on her twelve-year-old face. "Mom, you've given him plenty of time. Over a year! He's just not right for you. I could see it the other day, watching you ride. Your face—you weren't having fun."

I gazed at her, speechless.

"We should sell him to someone he'll fit with," she insisted, "and find a horse you can enjoy."

I turned back to the road, my mind racing. I had, in fact, been thinking these same thoughts myself. I had recently written about the tell-tale feelings that indicate when a split with your equine partner may be in order. Anger and frustration were two of the emotions, and I had been experiencing both of them.

My gelding, an older guy, just wasn't as responsive as I needed him to be. Following the article's advice, I had put him in training. Though the trainer was having some success in getting his weight back over his hindquarters (his engine) and lightening his forehand for balance and ease of changing directions and gaits, he was still "heavy in the bridle"—leaning hard on the bit whenever I rode him.

Dealing with this issue had become a drag, literally and figuratively. Plus, I wasn't sure I was up to the challenge of "fixing" him. As the article suggested, I also felt guilt whenever I contemplated not sticking it out. Killian was a lovely horse in many ways, kind-hearted and even-tempered. I hated giving up on him.

But Sophie had nailed it—riding him just wasn't fun anymore. And, at that point in my life, given the limited time I had for riding, it really did need to be fun rather than simply an ongoing, daunting challenge.

"Mom?" Sophie wanted my response.

"Well," I began, then hesitated again. I saw her in my mind's eye, tiny atop her nine-hand "starter pony," a Miniature Horse she had just before we acquired Diamond, her first "real pony." Wasn't that just yesterday, when I had to explain why she couldn't give Smoky a "haircut," and why he didn't need a bath *every* day?

And now here she was, advising me.

I shouldn't have been surprised. This is, after all, the kid who programmed, "Welcome, Mom – Don't Worry!" into my cell phone's welcome screen to allay my technophobia, knowing I would never have the savvy to do it myself. She takes care of me that way.

I glanced over at her and smiled.

"Honey, you may be right."

"We'll find him a good home," she went on, "with someone who'll love him. And there's a better horse for *you* out there waiting, somewhere."

I smiled, thinking back to when we had shopped for a larger pony to replace Smoky. We had brought a cute little sorrel Welsh mare home on trial, but it hadn't worked out, and Sophie, then eight, had been heartbroken.

"Don't worry, honey," I told her at the time. "Your real pony is still out there somewhere, waiting for you."

Now she was reassuring me of the same thing.

In the end, I did find a more suitable home for Killian. That cleared the deck for me to acquire Falcon, a sweet Paint mare who boosted my confidence. On her, I was able to continue the mother-daughter horse-life adventure I so loved—thanks to the good advice of my very own personal equine advisor.

Chapter 23: Staying One Step Ahead

"Hmph! I'm mad at Brego!"

My daughter sat across from me in the truck cab, arms crossed, frowning. We were on our way to a riding lesson with her pony in tow.

"Why, honey?" I could tell she was more hurt than angry.

"When I went to get him this morning, he turned away and wouldn't let me catch him. Then he ran around the paddock about a million times before I *could* catch him. He knows better than that! He was a bad boy."

I pictured the scene. The look of surprise, then frustration, on my twelve-year-old's face as her usually submissive gelding took off on a tear. And a look of high mischief in the pony's eye as he put his dollop of Arabian blood on full, glorious display—tail pluming, neck arching, nostrils blown full as in those thrilling pen-and-ink drawings of *The Black Stallion*.

I held back a smile. As a parent, I recognized this as a "teaching moment"—if I could manage not to blow it.

"He doesn't normally do that, does he?" I asked innocently.

"No, and that's what makes me so mad—I was afraid we wouldn't get him loaded in time, and we'd be late to the lesson. Of all the bad times to be naughty!"

Consternation clouded her face. Sophie, who sets timers for herself to be punctual for important events, really would hate to be late to her lesson. "Don't you think it was maybe precisely because you do have a lesson today that he decided he didn't want to be caught?"

"How would he know that, Mom?"

I took one hand off the wheel and waved it through the air. "A bunch of ways. He sees you in those clothes, the ones you always wear to lessons. You're carrying his good halter, instead of the old one. You're seriously intent on catching him—after all, you don't want to be late, right?"

"Yeah," she admitted.

"So, he adds all that up and decides, 'Nope. Don't wanna get caught, go into the trailer, go to that other place, and work my fanny off.' Remember what natural horsemanship tells you," I went on, referring to training method that emphasizes the horse's point of view.

"Horses generally prefer not to work—just like us. Brego thought maybe he'd arrange it so he wouldn't get caught today, so he could avoid all that exercise."

Sophie looked over at me, weighing my words. I pressed my advantage.

"In the pasture, did you really think you could catch him if he didn't want to be caught?"

"Well, no. But what else could I do?"

"Refuse to play his game! He's using his brain—small compared to ours—to try to outsmart you. If you start chasing after him, you're playing on his terms, which gives him the upper hand. A better idea is to use your own great, big brain to change the game."

I glanced over at her. She was frowning in concentration. Like any kid, she wanted to outsmart me, but she was beginning to realize it wasn't going happen—this time.

"How would it have been different," I continued, "if the moment he turned away from you, you'd stopped, walked back to the barn, and gotten a handful of grain?"

Sophie smiled sheepishly. "He'd have come right to me."

"Yes! So it never would have gotten to the running-around part. That's actually your mission, as the smarter of the two of you. To arrange it so Brego *wants* to do what you want him to do."

Sophie nodded her head and smiled. I smiled back. As I did, I realized that this set-them-up-to-succeed strategy—assuming you can remember it when you need it—isn't just for horses. It works nicely with kids, too.

Chapter 24: The Waiting Game

"Can you get a urine sample?"

It was my veterinarian on the phone, catching me by surprise.

"I think so," I replied, wondering how I would accomplish this with a pony.

"It takes some patience," he added.

Oh. I envisioned myself sitting out in the pasture all day, waiting for nature to call, knowing that a watched pot never boils.

Still, I would try. Brego, my daughter's black gelding, had turned out to be a wonderful child's mount. He had safely carried her over many a jump and through all sorts of horseback activities. Although he didn't seem sick, he was urinating frequently, and the vet wanted to rule out anything serious. That's what the urinalysis—and a blood panel—would do.

The vet would draw the blood when he arrived; my job in the meantime was to capture the urine. Somehow.

I grabbed a clean jar and a notebook, and headed out to the horse pasture. I needed the notebook because, as bad luck had it, I was on deadline for an assignment that very morning. Sitting out in the pasture, I would need to finish up my work the old-fashioned way—by hand, on the notebook.

Anything for you, Brego.

I found a box to sit on and drew it up in the shade of the horses' loafing shed. The May day was pleasant, warm but not hot. The sun shone, birds chirped. I began to feel this might be the perfect place to work.

Until the animals crowded in.

First, it was Brego himself, checking me out. His soft, whiskery muzzle traced a line from my notebook, up my arm, over my head, back to the notebook. His breath, warm and fragrant, blew over me. Finally, his nosing finished, he headed back to his stall, where the remaining bits of his breakfast hay beckoned.

I glanced back at the last paragraph on my notebook. Where was I? Before I could proceed, Buddy, our Saanen goat, wandered over to begin his own in-your-face investigation. I pondered the options for shooing him away, none of them promising.

Then, abruptly, the pony walked out of his stall, found a comfortable spot near his manure pile, and "dropped" (a horseman's term for preparing to urinate). I scrambled for the jar, then stood at hand, poised for action.

False alarm. Brego wandered back into his stall, swishing his tail.

I returned to my sitting box, where Buddy was nibbling a corner of my notebook. "Go, Buddy!" I commanded, pointing to a far corner of the pasture. He regarded me with calm, quizzical eyes, like a biologist examining a newly discovered species.

"Buddy, *go!*" I repeated. His amber eyes closed slowly, then opened; nothing else moved.

As if to help, the pony stepped over to us and pinned his ears, sending Buddy scurrying. Then Brego began a new, more careful inspection of me. His manner said, "You must have treats, somewhere." Finding none, he walked away, then paused. I jumped up, jar in hand. The goat returned to head me off, the hair along his back standing in a rigid line. (Buddy always fancied himself the horses' protector. In this moment, he saw me as an aggressor who must be stopped.)

"Buddy!" I exclaimed, pushing him away, my eyes fixed on Brego. The pony stood indecisively for a moment, then strolled over to the water tank for a drink.

Newly hopeful, I returned to my box and sat down. It couldn't be long now. Brego headed back over to conduct his third inspection, muzzle dripping water. I shooed him away.

Then Killian, my own riding horse, emerged from his stall, sighing contentedly. He glanced about, assessing the situation, then walked to the water tank for a drink.

The goat, meanwhile, was rooted at my elbow, his head about level with mine. He urped, flexed his jaw, and began chewing the cud he had just brought up from his gut. I watched, fascinated, as his weird little teeth moved back and forth.

Brego wandered over and tried to lip my hair. I waved him back into his stall. He came out again, determined to wipe his now-muddy muzzle on my manuscript. He succeeded. Then he walked forward, sniffing the ground purposefully. *This is it!* I jumped up, dropped the notebook, grabbed the jar, pushed the goat away.

Nature did indeed call, but it wasn't what I had been waiting for. Brego stepped away from the moist, fragrant pile and returned to his stall. I sat back down and tried to concentrate on my work. For a moment, I did. Then I heard the sound of urinating. I was missing it! I leaped and turned, and...it was Buddy, not Brego.

I sat back down. Time passed. I frowned at my smudgy notebook.

Then, at last, it happened. Brego walked out, paused, and assumed the position. I jumped up one final time, gripping the jar. The stream began; I caught some of it, marveling at its force. (Mental note: Next time, taller jar.)

When the vet arrived later that day, I presented the jar with pride. Later still, I learned the tests were normal; the pony, fine. I went on to finish the manuscript I had been working on, then smiled as I tucked away the slobber-smeared notes that became the basis for my next story—and this chapter.

Chapter 25: 'Sadly Outgrown'

It finally happened. My daughter, Sophie, began outgrowing her good pony, Brego. He of the large, kind eye and can-do spirit. The willing lesson mount, show-ring partner, and river-swimming buddy. Her four-legged best friend.

It wasn't a red alert just yet. At 14.1 hands, Brego would be able to carry my daughter for a while yet. But Sophie had just turned 13, and the time was coming when the pony would become, in that ubiquitous, wholly inadequate phrase, "sadly outgrown."

And then what?

My family had faced this dilemma before. When Sophie outgrew her smaller pony mare, Diamond, we wound up loaning her to a friend who used her to teach horsemanship to a young child she mentored.

A perfect solution! Only, as I told Sophie at the time, we couldn't keep collecting horses indefinitely, as if they were Breyer models.

And yet, as the time approached, even thinking of selling Brego gave me stomach flips. Especially as I had just edited, for an equine magazine, a special report on the debate over the slaughter of horses for human consumption.

The dilemma is this: You can sell your good horse to a good home, and all will be well for a time. But, eventually, the horse may get sold again, and possibly again, and sooner or later you'll lose track of him. One day, he'll be old and possibly no longer sound for riding. Then what will happen to him?

That's the quandary a caring horse owner faces. Some animal-rights groups say the solution is you shouldn't ever sell the horse in the first place. They say don't acquire a horse unless you plan to keep him for life. It's the standard we try to apply to cats and dogs (not very successfully, though, according to animal-shelter statistics), and these advocates believe we should apply it to horses, as well.

But horses aren't companion animals in the same way cats and dogs are. Legally, they're classified as livestock. Horses do become companions, of course. But they're also their owners' partners in recreation and competition. We ride and drive them in horse shows; they carry us across the countryside on trail rides.

And, sometimes, we find that a horse we've acquired isn't suitable for us, after all. He may be too much for us to handle, or not athletic enough for what we hope to do with him, or simply not an appropriate, safe match in some other way. That's when we're likely to sell him to someone for whom he *will* be a good match.

But what about later? Will he someday face that "uncertain fate," the euphemism we use for slaughter? People opposed to slaughter have always believed making it illegal solves the dilemma. But with slaughter banned in the United States, will the horse you sell today wind up eventually neglected by someone who can't or won't care for him properly?

Or, worse, sent to a less regulated, less humane slaughterhouse in Mexico?

These are grinding questions. Fortunately, efforts to find solutions have been in progress for some time, including clearinghouses that help connect horses in need of homes with rescue facilities or others willing to take them in (see ahomeforeveryhorse.com).

Beyond that, there's much that horse owners can do to make sure our own good horses never fall on hard times. For starters, we can avoid breeding horses unless we know the resulting foals will be wanted and marketable. When we find ourselves with a no-longer-needed horse, we can lease or loan him out instead of selling him outright. Or we can sell him with a buy-back right of first refusal. With the latter option, you'll know if he ever goes up for sale again, so at least you can keep track of him and perhaps help to find him another good home.

In this way, though our four-legged partners become "sadly outgrown," they never become forgotten.

And Brego? He became my family's final pensioner, living out his years on our property with a succession of goats as companions. Whenever I see his handsome old face, now turning white with age, I think what a perfect solution this is—for all of us.

Part V. Bleats & Bells: Goat Capers

"If you're short of trouble, take a goat."
~ Finnish Proverb

Goats are oddly appealing creatures. In my experience, they're smarter than horses, but less obliging. They do what they want to do, period. And they don't miss a trick. If you make a mistake—say, leave an opened gate unattended for a split second—they'll capitalize on it. They're out and gone, before a horse has even raised his head to look.

Quick and clever, goats can make us humans feel a bit thick. When you look a goat in the eye, you get the distinct feeling the goat is looking back just as curiously at you, wondering what's going on in your head.

Goats are the smart-alecky class clowns that can't stop pushing your buttons. Sometimes it makes you want to scream…but mostly you can't stop loving them for it.

Chapter 26: Kidding Around

B uddy began his life as part of a local teen's 4-H goat project. We bought him as a weanling to be a pasture mate for Sophie's pony, Diamond. Back then, Diamond was the only horse on our property. Being a herd animal, she needed a buddy. The little goat, whom our then nine-year-old daughter named so appropriately, filled the bill to perfection.

Goats make excellent companions for horses. The two species have often been paired, and they share considerable history together. The term "to get one's goat" (meaning to make one angry or upset) traces to the days when goats were common at racetracks as calming companions to high-strung Thoroughbreds. The act of stealing the goat from a rival's barn would unnerve the rival's horse. This underhanded tactic, in turn, spoiled all prospects of that horse winning a race. Goats can be serious business.

Our own first goat was about six months old when he came to live with us. Recently neutered (which made him a *wether*), he was small, white, and utterly irresistible. A purebred Saanen (a popular dairy breed from Switzerland), he had the docile temperament and mellow nature of his tribe.

And cute, omigosh! His ears flopped forward earnestly over a sweet face; his caramel-colored eyes followed you everywhere with a friendly, knowing look.

Though timid at first, Buddy quickly came to appreciate Diamond's near-maternal attentions. He also bonded with us human folk, especially Sophie, to her delight. She played what she called "goat tag" with him—tapping him and then scurrying off. He would dart after her, turning when she turned, jumping when she jumped, putting on the skids when she stopped. He was usually mannerly, though, and never tried to butt her with his bony (though de-horned) head.

Whoever coined the verb "to caper" must have had young goats in mind. At times, Buddy bounded four-legged like a deer, only laterally, coming at you broadside in great leaps. Next came a stint of inside-out bucking, then he would cap the performance with tough-guy head slinging. It was as though he were saying, "There! How was *that*?!"

He could be possessive, though. Once, when we borrowed two female goats to keep him company while Diamond was away at the trainer's barn, he put on a display of jealousy at the water tank. I came to the fence to fill the tank, and the two does came running to greet me, bleating loudly in their Nubian voices.

Buddy glanced up from the brush he was nibbling (another advantage of goat-owning) and bounded after the does, shaking his head in an I-mean-business way.

"Hey!" blared his body language. "This is *my* human!" He leaped onto the 18-inch-high cement block that's the foundation for the water tank, whirled to face the does, and reared, Black-Stallion-style.

Then, still balancing on his hind legs, he launched himself down at them, a fearless, 50-pound kamikaze. As they scattered, he scooted after them, thrusting his head this way and that, buttressing his "she's mine" message. I was flattered, to be sure, but also laughing so hard I wound up spraying myself with the water hose.

Buddy added whimsy to our trail rides, too. Where we live, neighbors are literally few and far between, so we sometimes let him tag along when we ventured out. My husband, watching us go, once remarked that we looked like some odd variation of the *Incredible Journey* threesome—Sophie on Diamond, Buddy scampering alongside, me trailing on foot.

We had a great time, though. Sophie, delighted by these outings, would chatter nonstop. Buddy would zigzag down the trail, snacking on the scenery. Diamond would step out alertly, furry ears pricked, behaving like the good pony she was.

I, meanwhile, had to pinch myself, often. Is a woman of my age allowed to have this much fun? I guess so—if she's lucky enough to have horses and kids of both types.

Chapter 27: That Old Goat

When our purebred Saanen goat, Buddy, was a yearling kid, I noted that he had a docile temperament and mellow nature, and was mannerly.

Mannerly—ha! Can't believe I actually said that.

That small, adorable kid soon matured into what you could only call "an old goat"—a title that has nothing to do with his age. In fact, Buddy clarified for me where the term "old goat" comes from, to describe an irascible, unrepentant old coot. Regardless of age.

That was Buddy.

He even looked the part. He had a potbelly and scraggly hair all over. His face, once cute and babyish, had become big and bony. His little white teeth were weirdly humanlike, and he had a ridiculously long, pointy beard. A *goatee*.

Did I say his eyes were knowing? Make that "knowing he was driving me crazy." When I was at the pasture gate to fetch one of the horses, he was there, too. His timing was flawless; his positioning, exact. He blocked my entrance, bristling with attitude: *Just try to make me move.*

A brisk "Get!" and a wave of the hand will step a horse right back.

But not Buddy. That approach just made him laugh his deranged little laugh. (I couldn't actually hear it but I knew he was doing it. I was sure of it.)

When he was a kid, I found his possessiveness charming. When he once chased off a couple of visiting goats from the water tank I was filling, I was convinced his body language said, "Back off—she's mine." Meaning me. I was actually flattered!

I soon realized it had nothing to do with me. He was just hogging the water—and showing off.

His possessiveness soon encompassed the horses, which led to an annoying strategy at the gate. Buddy did *not* want me to come in to get one of *his* horses. When I forced my way in anyway and haltered my Paint mare Falcon, he used his signature blocking maneuver to try to keep me from leading her out.

You know how a motorist cuts you off by pulling right in front of you? Buddy did that. As I tried to make my way back to the gate, horse in hand, he angled his trajectory perfectly to step diagonally in front of me, over and over.

"Buddy!"

It was useless.

And after he had bumped into me the umpteenth time, I knew I would be covered in poison oak. (That was his one remaining virtue: He ate the stuff. But then he lost those brownie points by rubbing the rash-inducing oil onto us.)

As irritating as he was with us, he was ten times worse with a stranger. One time, a neighbor and his two small children came over to feed our animals while we were away overnight. After placing hay in the mangers, the neighbor decided to walk home through our pasture, a more direct route than back down the driveway. It never occurred to him this might be hazardous, because all the animals would be busy eating dinner, right?

Not Buddy. Being a goat means never passing up an opportunity to be a pain—even if it means interrupting a meal. He traipsed after our neighbor and his children, trying to insert himself into their midst until finally the guy had to scoop up his terrorized little ones and dash for the fence line.

I only hope he wasn't screaming in terror.

When Buddy was a kid, I used to love how he would accompany my daughter and me on trail rides, skittering about and snacking on the scenery as he went. *So* cute, etc., etc.

Before long, though, we were leaving that cloven-hooved nuisance at home when we went riding—though that was no guarantee he wouldn't somehow crash the party.

On one ride, Sophie on Brego and I on Falcon were about a mile down the road when suddenly both our horses spooked. We pulled them around, thinking, *Deer? Bobcat? Jackrabbit? COUGAR?!*

Nope, just Buddy, sneaking up behind us. We never did figure out how he got out of the pasture. Demonic powers are a possibility.

Why did we keep him, you may wonder? I wondered that, too. I guess the answer was that we still, somehow, loved that old goat.

Chapter 28: Get My Goat—Please

"*B uddy!*"

Back in the day, on any morning around animal-breakfast time, that would be me, yelling at our goat.

Buddy, our white Saanen wether, had been in our family since he was a kid—an adorably cute kid, as I've noted in earlier chapters. But, as I've also noted, he aged from a sweet kid into an *old goat* in the fullest sense of the epithet.

He became cranky. Ill-behaved. A bit like a third-world dictator—set in his ways, a little loony, impossible to reason with. A tyrant.

To be honest, it wasn't really his fault. Though we had owned him since he was an impressionable youngster, we had never given him a lick of training. Despite this, he still led (reluctantly) by his collar, and stood (defiantly) to have his hooves trimmed.

So I suppose I shouldn't have complained so much.

But...he was such a bully!

One holiday period, for example, he terrorized my sister and brother-in-law when they came to gather greenery on our property. Sherry and Gene host a magnificent prime-rib dinner every Christmas, and that year, Sherry wanted to use clippings from our pyracantha bushes and gray pine trees. (The pyracantha berries can pass for holly berries; pair them with pine boughs, and you have a splendid table arrangement.)

So there the two of them were, on our property, clippers in hand, when they were set upon by Dear Leader in a goatee. (I should explain that I used to open a goat-sized pasture gate every morning to allow Buddy out to nibble the brush outside the pasture. I forgot this detail when I told Gene and Sherry, "Sure— c'mon over any time.")

Gene was trying to put some clippings onto the open tailgate of his truck when Buddy sidled up and grabbed a branch with his weird little teeth. A pulling match ensued; Gene, a strong fellow, was able to wrest away the clippings. But then he tried to keep the goat backed off by pushing on Buddy's knobby-but-hornless head.

This wounded Buddy's dignity. He drew himself up to his full height, adding an inch by erecting a ridge of wiry hair down his topline. Then he reared and hopped a few times on his hind legs—goatspeak for, "Put up your dukes, punk."

That did it for Gene and Sher. They grabbed what cuttings they could, threw them on the tailgate, and dove into the truck.

"I couldn't get the door open fast enough," Sherry told me, later. "That goat was *right there.*"

As Gene fired the ignition, Buddy kept snatching clippings from the tailgate.

"Hey! This is MY FOOD!" seemed to be his general message, not exactly in keeping with the spirit of the holidays. But that was Buddy. The original Scrooge.

He started misbehaving with the horses, too. We adopted Buddy in the first place to be a companion animal to Diamond, our pony at the time. Later he became pals with Brego, my daughter's larger Pony Club pony, and then Redford, a gelding I was boarding temporarily for a friend. When Redford returned home, it was back to Brego and Buddy only.

"Just the two of you," I told them. "Friends and amigos. Buddies!"

Well, not exactly. By the morning after Redford's departure, Buddy had turned into a despot. When I came out to feed, the pony wasn't waiting patiently in his favorite stall as per normal. Instead, he was running from one stall to the other.

At first, I thought he was just feeling his oats, so to speak, in advance. Then I noticed that each time he entered a stall, Buddy darted in after him and booted him out, deploying the same tactics he had used on Sherry and Gene.

"Buddy, *quit!*" I commanded, to no effect. I put Brego's grain in the goat-proof manger, and the pony—fully four times the size of the goat—finally bulled his way into the stall, put his head down, and began eating.

As I watched through the stall's window, I couldn't see Buddy, but every two or three seconds I saw evidence of him, as Brego's body shuddered with the impact of the goat's head slamming into his shoulder.

Not a nice way to eat your breakfast.

I always found myself making allowances for Buddy, hoping his behavior would smooth out over time. But I do remember wishing every once in a while that someone would come *get my goat*—permanently.

Chapter 29: Replacing Buddy

A nimals break your heart. They do it when they leave us, and sometimes when they arrive as well—as this tale will tell. They never do it purposefully, of course, or even consciously. They're completely innocent.

But your heart breaks all the same.

We lost Buddy, our curmudgeonly Saanen goat, two weeks before Christmas one year. For as long as we had owned him—since he was a kid—I had been on the lookout for symptoms of a blocked urethra, a condition not uncommon in neutered male goats. Though Buddy could be a cantankerous old thing, I couldn't bear the thought of him straining unsuccessfully to urinate, ultimately dying of a ruptured bladder.

As it turned out, we were relatively lucky. Buddy avoided this condition until the age of thirteen, somewhat elderly for a goat, and we caught it before he was in extreme discomfort.

So it became a matter of euthanizing him before the blockage could cause real misery. It felt like the right thing to do, but also the wrong thing, as anyone who has euthanized a beloved animal knows.

When we made that hard decision, Buddy was already partly anesthetized, as our veterinarian had been trying unsuccessfully to remove the blockage. During this procedure, the pony Brego,

Buddy's pasture mate, had stood nearby in his stall, watching quietly. But as the vet injected the substance that ended Buddy's life, Brego charged out of his stall and began running up and down the fence line, looking at his friend and nickering in alarm.

It was uncanny and heartbreaking.

We buried Buddy on our property the next day, then began searching for a new companion for Brego. The pony, then twenty-three, enjoyed good health; we expected he could be around another decade or more. It's not fair to keep a herd animal on his own, but I did wonder how—if you keep acquiring a replacement companion for the remaining animal—you ever wind up with zero pensioners.

Setting aside that quandary, we concentrated on finding a female goat this time (to avoid any further blockage problems). A 4-H family looking to downsize their herd offered to let us adopt a LaMancha female, about six years old and large enough to pal around with a pony. An online search informed us this is the only goat breed developed in the United States. LaManchas are also unique for having little or no outside ears, which gives them a sleek, baby-seal look. They're relatively quiet, too, like the Saanen and unlike the Nubian (notorious for its loud, bawling bleat).

The family delivered this goat to us on Christmas Eve. We set her up in a pen apart from Brego to give the animals time to get acquainted without a skirmish. Her owners called her "Moo," a fragment of her registered name. She was black in front and white behind, and blessed with the gentle, cooperative nature characteristic of her breed.

As the father and son helped my husband, daughter, and me settle her in, Moo stood among us, looking from person to person intelligently, occasionally nibbling a bite of hay. She seemed perfectly at ease in her new surroundings.

"If you run into any problems," said the dad, "let us know, and we'll take her back." I felt virtually certain this wouldn't be necessary.

Then "her people" got in their truck and drove away. Like a toddler suddenly realizing she had been left with a sitter, Moo had a meltdown. She called after the truck frantically and sought to escape the pen, once even throwing herself desperately against the wire mesh.

The three of us watched in shock and dismay. My daughter and I, especially, were torn whenever the goat paused to gaze intently into our faces. Her manner seemed to say, "A human—yes. I want. But not *you*."

Meanwhile, the pony begged for Moo's attention. From the moment the goat had arrived, Brego showed keen interest. His intense, quizzical expression said, "Is it Buddy? No. Still—I love her."

He paced around the outside of Moo's paddock, *huh-huh-huh*-ing in his most appealing way, to no avail. The goat either ignored him, or scooted as far from him as possible.

This wasn't the cozy scene we had envisioned! But then Buddy had been a baby when we got him, whereas Moo was an adult.

"Give it time," my husband said.

So that's what we did, hoping for the best. Her owners mentioned before they left that two prior adoptions had failed. At the time, dazzled by Moo's sweet face, I had neglected to ask why. Before long, I began to suspect her separation anxiety had proved too heartbreaking for the earlier families to bear. After witnessing the depth of Moo's almost-human dismay, I could understand how that could be.

We continued to keep the two animals separate, allowing supervised "nose-touch" sessions to help them break the ice.

Moo began to seem a little less anxious each day, and Brego started settling down, too.

Still, each time we walked away from the barn and she called after us plaintively, it was pure anguish. And a reminder that what makes animals so dear to us is also the thing that can break our hearts.

Chapter 30: A Short, Sweet Life

It had definitely been a process.

When we adopted the LaMancha goat Moo to be a companion for our pony, we knew there would be an adjustment period. But we weren't expecting the goat to grieve so over the family she had left behind, and we certainly didn't think we would have to worry about the pony attacking the goat.

Here's what happened.

Brego showed interest in Moo from the start. She, by contrast, was interested only in humans, and clearly missing the ones she had left behind. We set her up in her own private quarters, a small pen with access to a run-in stall. Brego had access to the barn's other two stalls and pens, plus the five-acre pasture the barn is situated in.

Moo's unhappiness ate at us. We made her stall snug, adding an interior wall of straw bales to create a protected corner. My husband tacked up plywood as needed to cut down on drafts, and it consoled us to see Moo nestled in her deeply bedded corner.

What we really wanted, though, was to see her buddied up to Brego, as content in his company as Buddy, our previous goat, had been. But it wasn't happening. The pony spent most of his time loitering next to Moo's pen, his hooves wearing away the grass in that spot as he tried to get her attention. Over time, Moo stopped actively withdrawing from Brego, but neither did she cozy up to him. She seemed indifferent.

Though we watched her closely, we could never catch her eating any of the grass hay and alfalfa pellets we provided.

"At least she's not losing weight," observed our daughter, Sophie, home from college on break. We put out more hay and tried not to worry.

We also worked our plan. This was to arrange a little meet-and-greet between the two animals every day. The three of us—husband, daughter, and I—would halter the gelding, then let Moo out of her enclosure into the pasture at large. Mostly, she stuck by us, her replacement humans, rebuffing Brego. Meanwhile, he was keen on getting next to her—a little too keen, it seemed.

Sometimes when we would try to get them to touch noses, Brego would pin his ears, and I would wonder what *that* was about. Online searching led me to a story of an Appaloosa gelding that killed a goat. Could sweet Brego be harboring murderous intentions?

Ghastly thought.

We upped our vigilance. As the days went by, Brego became less intense and Moo even more relaxed. Finally we decided to test the waters by turning them out together—with us right there to mediate.

Sophie unsnapped the lead rope from Brego's halter. He took a step toward Moo, who retreated. Brego then pinned his ears, opened his mouth and—I swear I nearly fainted—lunged at her! She scooted away. Brego followed, mouth still agape.

As Sophie and I shouted and waved our arms, the pair circled back, and my husband was able to grab Brego's halter. Then we all just stood there.

Something about the way Brego had moved his head when he went after Moo rang a bell for me, but I didn't stop to think about it at the time. We all marveled, though, at how matter of fact Moo seemed in the moment, moving away from Brego, yes, but appearing only mildly upset about it. Certainly not as upset as we were. And Brego now seemed completely serene.

"We'll just give it more time," Hank said as we put Moo back into her pen. "A *lot* more time."

The holiday break ended and Sophie went back to school. I came up with an idea I thought might move the process along a little. We would confine Brego in one of his pens, so he'd have access only to it and the adjoining stall, and leave open the gate to Moo's pen so she would have access to the entire pasture. That way, she could wander about and control how much proximity she and Brego would have, and they would still always be separated by a fence.

Moo seemed to like this idea and went about exploring the area around the outside of Brego's pen. Brego did *not* like this arrangement, however. I didn't realize how much, though, until the next morning.

As I walked out to feed, I spotted Brego pacing the fence line in his pen. When Moo had returned to her own stall the night before, Brego—no longer able to go stand next to her pen—had become as restless as a mare kept from her foal. He must have been at it the whole night, too, because he looked as if he had dropped about 100 pounds.

"Brego!" I called to him. "What are you *doing?*" He took no notice and kept trudging back and forth, obsessively.

That led me to remember—bitterly—that the whole point of this enterprise had been to keep Brego from loneliness, to make him happy. Instead we were making him neurotic.

We shut Moo back into her pen and restored Brego's access to the pasture. More time, I told myself.

A few days later, I walked out to find both Moo and Brego in the pasture together—somehow, Moo had squeezed through her pen's gate. My heart quailed; then I realized they seemed perfectly fine. I walked down the fence line a bit and Moo followed me, at which point Brego charged after her.

I held my breath and prayed.

Brego galloped up to her and stopped. Then he put his head down and blew gustily through his nostrils, as if saying, "All righty, then!" After that, they both just stood there.

And that's when I realized it was going to be OK. I then remembered something about Brego and his former pasture-mate Redford. The two geldings would perform equine kabuki theater twice a day at feeding time. Each would grimace, pin his ears, and swing his hindquarters threateningly at the other, but they never actually touched.

It was all for show.

That's what my subconscious was telling me the first time Brego lunged at Moo—that he resembled a stallion snaking his head at a mare. Brego wasn't intending to hurt Moo, the single member of his "herd." He was just showing her who was in charge. And she was reading his body language much better than we were.

As time went on, Moo started calling her own shots. She hung out with Brego or retreated to her private quarters as she pleased. Brego gained his weight back, and he no longer seemed neurotic. They started forming a bond.

Then…tragedy struck. Moo was diagnosed with goat polio, a common metabolic disorder caused by a thiamine deficiency. Our vet treated her, but, to our shock and dismay, she didn't survive.

We were heartbroken, and so was the pony. In fact, Brego seemed even more distraught than when he had lost Buddy, his first goat companion. I thought perhaps this was because Moo was female, Brego had a strong herding instinct, and Moo was his "herd."

Only now she was gone, and we were back to the problem of a pony living on his own. With a heavy heart, I began a new search for a companion.

Chapter 31: The 'Streetcar' Girls

S ometimes heartache leads to renewed joy.

Our pony Brego had enjoyed two goat companions, first Buddy and then Moo. When we lost Moo to disease, we began looking for a new pasture-mate, trying to apply everything we had learned in our time as owners of goats.

This time, I decided we would seek out two doe goats. That way, they could keep each other company while they settled in, plus give Brego a larger "herd" to love and protect. And, being females, they wouldn't be subject to the blocked-urethra problem that had led to the demise of Buddy, our first goat.

Finding exactly what we wanted took time.

"Don't worry, Brego," I told the lonely pony at feeding time as the weeks, then months, ticked by. "Your new girls are coming."

Finally, a neighbor's tip pointed us toward a local 4-H family that had several Saanen does available. We chose a yearling and a three-year-old, both of them small, delicate, and pure white. They looked like albino deer.

The older one's name was Stella, so we christened the younger one Blanche. (Yes, in *A Streetcar Named Desire*, the *older* sister is Blanche, but no matter. It was close enough.)

On the day we brought the goats home, Brego greeted us at the gate—head up, ears forward, eyes riveted on the little newcomers. We bedded them down in their own pen with run-in stall, where they could get acquainted with their barn-mate from behind a safe fence.

Two weeks later, we tried putting them all together. As he had with Moo, Brego ran after each of the goats in turn, putting his head down and trying—unsuccessfully—to control their movements. They scampered away, but didn't seem alarmed.

We tried again a week later. This time, Brego accepted his new companions calmly, nudging them gently with his nose. Before long, the two little goats were following him everywhere he went, checking out the larger pasture and everything in it.

Blanche, the younger, sprightlier one, delighted in jumping up on anything available, sticking her landings like an Olympic gymnast—even on surfaces as narrow as four inches. This was adorable at first, but then turned problematic. Blanche would zip into Brego's stall, leap up into his manger to reach his corner feed tub, and scarf up his pellets right under his nose.

"Brego!" I scolded. "Don't let her do that! Chase her away!"

He declined to do so, and I could just imagine his internal dialogue. *Don't chase the goats. Do chase the goats. Make up your mind, already.*

A better solution, my husband and I decided, was to build a barrier from which Brego—but not Blanche—could access the tub. This strategy worked…for about ten minutes. Then Blanche upped her game. Positioning herself as before in the manger, she leaped in a curved trajectory to land—somehow—on the top of the barrier, where she clung with her nimble hooves while plunging her head down into the feed tub.

Really, you can't imagine how strong a little goat is until you've tried to pull her head out of a feed bucket.

Hank got out his tools and went back to work, and this time the reinforced barrier held Blanche at bay. The goats had access only to their own scoop of goat chow, in their own stall, plus as much grass hay as they could eat.

Yet, in those early weeks, when I would depart after feeding them and the pony, their plaintive calls would follow me as I walked back to the house. Saanens have nice voices, so their tender-yet-insistent bleating was heart-wrenching. It was the sound a mama goat might make if she knew her baby was being led to slaughter.

Of course, what they actually were saying was simply "more food!"—and this, right after consuming a full serving of goat chow, and with nice grass hay waiting in their manger. (Not to mention Brego's hay, which they would also nibble on.)

And that's how it goes with goats, from my experience. Either they're delighting you with their adorable faces and endearing antics, or tearing your heart out when they're ill or unhappy or wailing for something they want.

Not terribly unlike human kids, come to think of it.

Fortunately, the begging behavior stopped when Stella and Blanche learned it didn't net them more grain. At feeding time, they would scoot into their stall, gobble their grain, then scamper out again, racing around the larger pen in joyful anticipation of treats. These I would sometimes set out on the cement block that supports the water trough, causing more capering plus jumping up and down on the block. With Blanche, the downward jumps would sometimes occur sideways, goat-kamikaze style, which brought bittersweet memories of the days when our first goat, Buddy, was just a kid.

Eventually, I affixed a little bell to each doe's collar, which means all this activity created a tinkling concerto I came to cherish. It sounded like the shepherds-in-the-field portion of old Christmas carols. Ambrosia for the ears.

And good for the heart.

Part VI: Animal Wisdom: What We Learn

Until one has loved an animal,
a part of one's soul remains unawakened.
~ Anatole France

Animals live close to the earth. They're engaged in the essential business of living, an art we humans easily lose touch with these days. We're stretched thin trying to attend to too many bids for our attention, many of them seeming extra-urgent by the insistence of devices delivering endless texts, posts, alerts, emails.

Animals remind us that the basics of life matter far more than this technological treadmill. They guide us back to the natural world, the one we long for—often without even realizing it—when we get too far drawn into the vortex of life as it is in the twenty-first century.

Animals represent simple, eternal virtues: living in the moment, honoring each day, tending to the bonds that make life meaningful. They stick by their friends, and they find ways to live peaceably in groups. By the simple fact of their own true natures, our four-legged friends challenge us to take a page from their humble books…and become better humans in the process.

Chapter 32: Four-Legged Teachers

I was on my way back downstairs to my home office after lunch. My little dog, Sadie, was sitting on the landing between floors, watching my approach. As usual, she had anticipated my next move and was already there, waiting for me to catch up.

As I reached her, I bent down on impulse and stroked her soft, caramel-colored coat, running my hand from the top of her little domed head to the base of her plumy tail. All twelve-plus inches of her.

"Good dog!" I told her. "You're *such* a good dog. Mother loves you."

This random, unasked-for attention electrified her. She jetted down the last bank of stairs and, dropping her hind end for speed, sprinted around the ground-floor level. Skidding around the edge of the sofa, she gunned it down the sofa's long side.

She ended this supercharged romp by springing up onto an overstuffed chair and propping herself to emit one sharp, joyful bark.

Watching her, I had three thoughts. The first was *Wow. That sure got a response.* The second was, *I really should do that more often— tell her how I feel about her.*

And the third was, *Actually, I should do that more often with everyone I love, animal and human. It costs nothing yet does so much for them...and for me.*

Smiling, I realized I had learned yet another valuable lesson from one of my animals. These lessons are a common occurrence, and I've accumulated a lot of them over the years.

Such as, Life is good. Mornings are great. Wear your heart on your sleeve. Enjoy your food.

Actually, when it comes to wearing your heart on your sleeve, dogs are the champions. No one is better at unconditional love. Dogs love in the manner all the great books, including the Bible, tell us we should: constantly, generously, with no regard to whether the affection is earned or deserved—or returned.

In loving so abundantly, dogs set a standard we humans find difficult to follow. Though we certainly can try.

Horses teach great lessons, too. They're especially good on topics of teamwork and cooperation. In the type of riding I've enjoyed, a challenging goal is establishing the right kind of connection from your hands to the horse's mouth, via the reins. In dressage, that connection is supposed to be soft yet constant, a bit like holding hands.

When you do it properly (in concert with the right use of your seat, weight, and legs, mind you), the horse will come "on the bit"—reaching for and maintaining an elastic contact with your hands while flexing softly at the jaw and rounding through the back.

The natural tendency of a rider striving for this effect is to pull back on the reins to draw the horse's head into the correct position. This is dead wrong. Also wrong is seesawing the reins or bumping them. There are any number of incorrect methods, most of which I've resorted to over the years with predictably disappointing results.

But here's what my Paint mare, Falcon, has taught me. When I'm trying to get her to soften a little, to make her connection with my hands lighter while maintaining the desired flexion, *I* must do what I want *her* to do. Soften.

I ease my hold on her mouth by moving one hand slightly forward for a moment. And when I do that, it's amazing, because she "softens" right back to me.

I give, she gives.

If instead I follow my instincts and try to pull her head back, she responds in kind. I pull against her, she pulls against me. Pursued over time, this approach produces a hard-mouthed horse that can *really* pull on you. And is no longer fun to ride.

But...when I give, she gives. It's like magic.

And it's a lesson I've found applies to humans as much as to horses.

Humans like my daughter. I've learned that when I'm trying to nudge her in a particular direction, force—even gentle force—is generally counterproductive. But if I take the pressure *off* at just the right moment—that is, if I "give" just a little—then she'll typically give right back, while maintaining the connection between us that's so important to me.

Take piano lessons, for example, which she had from age eight to seventeen. Like all piano students, Sophie wasn't fond of practicing. My job was to remind her about it and, if need be, encourage her to plop herself down at the piano bench and just do it.

Sometimes, though, when she was feeling the pressure of other things she should or could be doing (homework, exercise, watching YouTube videos), she balked. At this point, if I gently encouraged her (that is, took up on the reins a bit), she sometimes resisted (that is, leaned into the bit instead of softening).

Occasionally she would blurt out, "I hate piano! I want to quit."

At that point I had two options. One was to say, "You *will* practice, and now. End of discussion." This was the equivalent of pulling back on the reins, hard.

The other option, the one I learned from my mare, was to do the opposite. To soften and to give, thereby taking the pressure off for a moment. "Well, it's up to you. If you don't want to play piano, you can quit."

This provided just the space she needed to realize that she actually didn't hate piano and in fact enjoyed playing. So she would soften back to me and sit down to practice. (Maybe for just five minutes that day, but hey, it was a victory.)

I find this approach works with husbands, too. When I pull, my husband pulls back. When I give a little, he gives a little...and the connection is preserved.

It's useful, that lesson my mare taught me. As are the other lessons I've learned, and am still learning, from all my four-legged teachers.

Chapter 33: Curiouser and Curiouser

I t was so odd. It happened during my daily walk. I paused at the top of a hill and watched, dumbfounded, as a skunk hurried by me on the left side of the road, passing me just the way one car would pass another. Alert and wily as any wild creature, the skunk had to have seen or smelled me there on the road. Yet he marched right on by without varying his pace or even glancing in my direction.

I felt an eerie déjà vu, not for something from my own past, but for something I remembered from a children's story. The way that skunk hustled by me was exactly the way the White Rabbit hustled past Alice just before they both tumbled down the hole into Wonderland (in Lewis Carroll's classic 1865 novel). The skunk had no waistcoat or pocket watch, but he was hurrying along in the same single-minded way, sticking to the road as if he knew it was the quickest route from where he had been to where he was going.

I could almost imagine him muttering to himself ("Oh, dear! Oh, dear! I shall be late!") and reaching for his watch.

Mesmerized, I stared after the skunk as long as I could, until he crested the next rise and dipped out of sight. Then I hurried on to the top of the rise myself in an attempt to get another glimpse, wondering whether he would stick to the road long enough for me to do so.

He did. At the top of the rise, I spotted him halfway up the next hill, still on his side of the road, still hurrying. For no good reason, I began to imagine him as a *her*, anxious to reach her burrow and see what mischief the little ones had gotten into in her absence.

The skunk had become Mrs. Tiggy-Winkle, subject of the Beatrix Potter book of the same name, published in 1905. My vision of the skunk included an apron and striped petticoat, a little white cap, and a nose "sniffle, sniffle, snuffling" as she rushed up the road.

At this point, I should clarify that I had ingested nothing before my walk that afternoon other than my usual pick-me-up cup of coffee. These curious notions entered my mind for no reason other than the skunk's odd behavior. (And, I might add, because conjuring them up was fun.)

I race-walked to the top of the next rise, winding myself, but the skunk was nowhere to be seen. I couldn't tell if he had darted off the road and into a burrow or culvert, or was now just so far ahead I could no longer catch sight of him.

Deflated, I continued on for my usual distance, then turned for home. Daylight was fading, and I was pondering how best to share this bizarre skunk encounter with friends and family when something brought me up short.

It was diluted skunk-smell, the sort that's not at all offensive, and in fact sometimes reminds me of the aroma of boutique coffee beans. (Go figure.) I was catapulted into a third children's book, *The Wind in the Willows*, Kenneth Grahame's 1908 classic. I became Mole, only instead of catching a whiff of my old underground burrow, as he does, I was sniffing evidence that perhaps my skunk friend had left the road somewhere near this spot and found shelter.

For a moment, I wished I could indeed be like Mole, and follow my nose to find what I was scenting. Then I snapped to, realizing that stunt—assuming it were possible—would likely only result in my getting skunk-sprayed. (But not necessarily bitten. Contrary to popular belief, not all skunks appearing in the daytime are rabid. Some are just searching for food. Often to feed offspring.)

With that thought, I'm back in Beatrix Potter-land, imagining the skunk as a diligent, nurturing mother-creature. Perhaps I'll see one of her babies someday.

I'm anthropomorphizing, I know. So sue me.

Chapter 34: Battles and Skirmishes

I t was an alarming sight. The big red horse lunged at the smaller black one, ears pinned, teeth bared. The black horse stood his ground, bracing his legs and preparing for battle. Two handsome heads darted in and around as the animals feinted and dodged, seeking an opening. Necks snaked and twisted, muscles bulged, manes flew.

Dust rose from their scrambling feet.

It was an awesome display of fierceness and power.

"Brego! Redford! Knock it off!"

They stopped, but not because of my command. Their little drama had run its course. They stood quietly, complacent, even.

I shook my head and marveled to think that, in the nine months or so since the bigger horse, Redford, had been with us, neither gelding had sustained as much as a scratch. Their antics were all for show. Their routine was as choreographed and ritualized as kabuki theatre.

The skirmishes happened just before feeding time, twice a day. At all other times, you could find the two of them hanging out amiably, body language relaxed, tails swishing.

Sometimes, in the hottest weather, their little act was abbreviated. Each horse would toss his head and make a mean face at the other, but they didn't even move their feet.

"OK, you he-men," I would tease. "Come get your grub." Sometimes, as they walked into their stalls to eat, they would menace each other one last time for good measure, flaring their nostrils as they flipped their heads in each other's direction.

Are you lookin' at ME?!

On this day, Redford hiked up his hip and directed a hind hoof at Brego, but the punch was pulled, as per normal, and no contact was made.

"Quit!" I growled out of habit. But it was like telling the crickets not to chirp, the trees not to grow. Mealtime macho, even if only for show, is hardwired into horses.

It's a "battle" that must be fought, because Mother Nature says so.

There are other, grimmer battles taking place at her bidding, as well. Inside the barn, as I peel off flakes of hay and slip them into feed nets, I hear a loud buzzing. I turn to look. In a dusty spider web across one corner of the barn window, a fly is about to meet its end. Like Frodo in Shelob's lair, the fly is hopelessly trapped. Every effort to free itself only tangles it more tightly in the soft, sticky filaments of the web.

I can't bear to watch what comes next, even though killing flies is something I do routinely myself. This particular death, being bound inextricably and then pierced and sucked dry by the spider, is one of nature's most gruesome. Shuddering, I head out to fill the horses' water.

As I walk along the fence line toward the water tubs, I spy a baby jackrabbit scurrying back under cover of brush. He had been nosing about the water spigot, where there's a little drip. Seeing him reminds me of another grim battle, one I didn't witness but inferred from the evidence one hot summer day.

I had found a young jackrabbit drowned in the bottom of a water tub that had only about eight inches of water in it. The inside of the tub was covered with scratch marks. Thirsty, the immature rabbit must have fallen in while trying to reach the water, then been unable to hop out. Panicking, perhaps when one of the horses approached the tub, it may have overexerted itself trying over and over to jump out, then died from fright and exhaustion.

Had the jackrabbit just remained still with its head above water, I could have tipped the bucket and set it free. But that's not nature's way.

Thinking of the baby bunny I've just seen by the spigot, I retrieve an old plastic water dish left over from the time we found a feral cat and kitten in the barn. I dust it off, set it next to the horses' water tub and fill it with water. Maybe that will head off another desperate struggle.

Then again, if the bunny comes to rely on the water, and I forget to fill it, or if one of my cats happens to notice him frequenting the water dish and lies in wait....

I try not to think about it. Dramas like these—some real, others not; some won, others lost—take place every day. Nature is unrelenting that way.

Life is grand, yes, especially out in the country.

But it's not without its battles.

Chapter 35: Treating People Like Animals

"Rrrrrrrrrrrrrr...." The muffled, one-note growl came from my little dog, Sadie. She was struggling not to bark. She desperately wanted to voice her excitement (*birds out the window!*), but she knew I wouldn't approve.

We had been over this and, like most dogs, Sadie always wants to please. She tries to understand what I want, then do it—to the best of her ability.

Contrast that with the attitude of Leo, my male cat. He doesn't worry about what I want. He knows when I'm wanting him to go into "his" room for the night, but if he's not feeling it, he won't go. I have to chase him down, pick him up, and lug him into his boudoir. He commits other misdemeanors, too, such as tripping me and tracking in dirt.

But, true to his species, Leo just doesn't care if he's displeasing me. He loves me, yes—no doubt about that. Still, he's wired to do his own thing, regardless of me or anyone else.

And yet...I love both these pets, dearly and equally. True, I expect Sadie to behave in the ways she knows how, but I'm understanding when something's beyond her ken. And I give Leo a complete pass because I know he just doesn't get it, ever.

I love these animals unconditionally. I accept them just exactly as they are. That feels good for them, and for me—a win-win situation.

So my question is, Why is this so much harder to do with the humans in our lives? Why can't we accept *them* just as they are? Why do we persist in expecting change from them—even changes we know in our hearts they're not going to make?

Like solving the problem they keep telling us about. Or quitting the behavior that's putting their health at risk. Or refraining from teasing in that way we find so—gah!—irritating.

Or stopping with all the advice already, geez.

The late Hugh Prather, a writer of great wisdom, said, "The moment I want something from another person, my happiness is compromised."

To that I would add: their happiness, too. Which makes it a lose-lose situation.

The obvious solution, then, would be to give people the same break we give our pets. Just let them be themselves. Live and let live, and enjoy them anyway. It's less stressful. We do it naturally for animals, but resist it with humans. Yet it's so freeing to release ourselves from wishing things could be different.

"Today," wrote Prather, "I will observe that I survive just fine without my expectations being met."

In truth, most people are generally doing the best they can with what they've got. The more we can view them that way (which is exactly the way we view our pets) the kinder we can feel toward them.

Then, too, change is difficult in any event, and it comes only from within a person, never at the direction of someone else. Moreover, it's impossible to know the complex network of influences that cause someone to be as they are or do the things they do.

Often, what annoys one person may be something the other person ultimately has little or no control over.

So your best bet is just to shrug it off when your brother teases you. Or your spouse does that one thing you've asked him or her—more than once!—not to do. Or your co-worker is late to a meeting. Again.

Granted, it can be a challenge to "let it be." I know this from my own experience. What I find helps, often a lot, is to say to yourself, "That's just what he does." Or, "That's just what she does."

Then let it go. Don't hold "that" against them, whatever it is—just as you don't hold it against your cat when she drools on you, or your dog when he spills his water bowl. Again.

As the philosopher and psychologist William James observed, "The art of being wise is the art of knowing what to overlook."

By giving the people in your life the same leeway you give your pets, you can overlook a lot—and let it go.

Chapter 36: A Dog's Life...at 60

Sixty is a big birthday. Even we baby boomers, so fond of redefining age groups (*fifty is the new thirty*, and so on), find sixty problematic. It's hard to claim you're still middle-aged when you've reached this milestone. Sixty is senior-hood, or at least the gateway to it. All those discounts and whatnot.

I've been pondering all this ever since I turned sixty, some years ago. I try to concentrate on the things that can help you feel better about getting older. There's the obvious one, of course, involving the alternative to aging. No one prefers *that*.

But there's a sweeter one as well, and an example of it is looking up at me this very moment, as I type. It's my little dog, Sadie, she of the caramel-colored coat and large, liquid eyes and floppy ears—all of which make her look like a pint-sized "Lady" from *Lady and the Tramp*.

How does a pet help as we ease into those Golden Years? By giving us a preview of the aging process, plus pointers on how best to deal with it.

We first acquired Sadie as a pup—an adorable baby. My real baby, daughter Sophie, was twelve at the time, and both of us, plus Sophie's dad, loved doting on this impossibly cute little ball of fur. Sadie needed constant supervision, special food, and potty-training, not unlike a human infant.

Dogs' lives zip by much faster than humans' do, however. In an eye blink, Sadie was a young adult dog, delighting us with her personality and her antics. She was enthusiasm incarnate, and up for anything the family wanted to do, including long walks.

Now she's entering her own Golden Years. She's graying around her eyes and muzzle, and her joints sometimes ache.

Yet she doesn't waste a thought on that gray hair. Doesn't bother her a bit. And whenever her joints suggest that she stay home instead of going on a walk, she just stays home, simple as that.

She doesn't regret it, or think, "Oh, I'm getting old!"

She just does what feels right in the moment and doesn't worry about it.

Most of the time, she still feels like a pup, happy and playful. She maximizes the things she really likes to do, like hang out with her family, scarf her meals, chase her green ball, chew her chew-bones.

And, based on how she greets *every single day*, life is good for Sadie.

I suspect her admirable pattern will continue as she grows even older, and I'm definitely taking notes. I've always believed dogs can serve as role models for us, but this particular aspect of canine character hadn't occurred to me before I started noticing the graying of that dear little face.

I console myself with the thought that small dogs often live longer than larger ones, though I can't say for sure that will be true in her case. What I do know is that however old she becomes, she'll be making the most of her life every day. To paraphrase writer/philosopher Aldous Huxley, the secret of genius is to carry the spirit of a dog into old age, which means never losing your enthusiasm.

Sadie "knows" that. She'll be doing everything she's capable of doing, and enjoying it. She'll also be leaving behind everything she can't do, and not giving it a second thought.

She will, in other words, be living her fullest life possible, with enthusiasm.

And, following her lead, I hope to be doing the same.

ACKNOWLEDGEMENTS

René E. Riley, my editor and friend, without whose enthusiasm and unerring guidance this book literally would not have been possible.

My sister, novelist Caroline Fyffe, who blazed the trail and aided me generously at every step.

My other sisters, Shelly Forsberg, Sherry Harm, and Mary Forsberg Turner, for their love and support and for insisting that I share these stories.

Steven D. Price, for sharing his publishing acumen, which runs deep and wide.

Barb Crabbe, DVM, for her veterinary expertise and unfailing friendship.

Temple Grandin, PhD, for helping me understand animals better.

The friends, family, and colleagues who read chapters or otherwise encouraged me, whether they realized it or not: Jenny Baginski, Randy and Karen Barrow, Rich and Laura Bireley, Sandy Collier, Laurie Cooper, Sue Copeland, Chris Daley, Darrell Dodds, Mimi Escabar, Adam Fyffe, Matthew Fyffe, Phyllis Gray, Susan Harding, Gene Harm, Alana Harrison, Christie Hunt,

Patrick Ibarra, Lili Joy, Pat Lakey, Rosella Lane, Teresa Larson, Barbara Lemos, Gregg and Jolene Matson, Bill and Thel Miller, Elizabeth Mills, Wendy Moyland, Jaime O'Neill, Jennifer Paulson, Sue Pearson, Steve Pratt, Jeff and Cecille Presley, Travis Presley, Judy Quincy, Mike Raffety, Lewis and Chris Ridgeway, Martin and Nicole Ridgeway, Wendy Schultz, Wendy Camp Shelton, Emily Spillmann, Noel Stack, Juli S. Thorson, Bonnie Timmons, Rachel Tranum, Christine Trout, Kathleen Turney, Mike and Jan Turney, Susan von Borstel, Kathy Samboceti Withrow, Lorna Samboceti Wren, Paula Zdenek.

Most of all, my husband, Hank Meyer, and daughter, Sophie Elene Meyer, for sharing my life and helping to make moments worth writing about.

ABOUT THE AUTHOR

Jennifer Forsberg Meyer, an award-winning journalist and author, is a native Californian and lifelong animal enthusiast. In addition to *Friends With Four Legs*, she's written three horse-related books, including *The Performance Horse: A Photographic Tribute*, featuring images of the late David R. Stoecklein.

Her column, *The Rural Life*, is published monthly in print and online by *The Mountain Democrat* of Placerville, California.

Now retired from her position as senior editor with *Horse&Rider* magazine, Jennifer lives in the Sierra Nevada foothills with her husband, Hank, and assorted animals. The couple has one grown daughter, Sophie Elene.